PENGUIN BUSINESS

SUCCESSFUL INTERVIEWING

Jack Gratus was born and educated in South Africa, where he obtained his Bachelor of Arts and Bachelor of Law degrees. He spent a number of years travelling before settling in London. His interviewing skills were honed in a solicitor's practice in the City of London, which involved divorce and criminal work. Since the 1970s he has taught interviewing to journalists, researchers and public relations professionals. He also holds journalism and interviewing classes in London, and these are always heavily over-subscribed. With the publication of his first novel, *A Man in his Position* (1968), Jack Gratus began a career as a writer and in ten years produced four more novels and three non-fiction books. He has written for magazines and newspapers and has recently devised documentary features for the BBC, as well as writing a number of plays for Radio 4's *Saturday Night Theatre*. He is a member and former co-chairman of the Writers' Guild of Great Britain.

He is married to Christine Gray, a director of an international advertising agency, and has two sons by his first marriage.

JACK GRATUS

Successful Interviewing

HOW TO FIND AND KEEP THE BEST PEOPLE

OOO

THE BRITISH SCHOOL OF OSTEOPATHY,
1-4 SUFFOLK ST., LONDON. SW1Y 4HG
TEL. 01 - 930 9254-8

PENGUIN BOOKS

PENGUIN BOOKS

Published by the Penguin Group
27 Wrights Lane, London W8 5TZ, England
Viking Penguin Inc., 40 West 23rd Street, New York, New York 10010, USA
Penguin Books Australia Ltd, Ringwood, Victoria, Australia
Penguin Books Canada Ltd, 2801 John Street, Markham, Ontario, Canada L3R 1B4
Penguin Books (NZ) Ltd, 182–190 Wairau Road, Auckland 10, New Zealand

Penguin Books Ltd, Registered Offices: Harmondsworth, Middlesex, England

First published 1988
3 5 7 9 10 8 6 4

Filmset in Linotron Sabon by
Rowland Phototypesetting Ltd, Bury St Edmunds, Suffolk
Made and printed in Great Britain by
Cox & Wyman Ltd, Reading, Berks.

CONTENTS

ooo

Part 1: What is an Interview?

Part 2: The Interview Plan

Part 3: Summing Up

Part 1: What is an Interview?

INTRODUCTION

ooo

In organizations large and small, even those with personnel departments, managers often find themselves placed in the situation of having to interview members of staff or to recruit new staff. They do not regard themselves as trained interviewers, nor do they think of their work as being primarily concerned with interviewing, and yet, if they were to analyse their actual day-to-day activities, they would see that much of it involved interviewing of one kind or another.

Interviews are happening all the time in a wide variety of circumstances. They are not always formal occasions with the two participants facing each other, a desk between them, the interviewer surrounded by papers, the interviewee isolated in a straight-backed chair. They can – and do – take place at any time, anywhere. The foreman talking to a new worker on the shop floor to see how he's getting on in the new job is conducting an interview; the company director chatting to a worried executive in the lift about some family problem is conducting an interview; even the chairman of the board, when seeking information from another member of the board during a meeting, will be doing so probably through the medium of the interview.

Although there will be variations, of course, to suit the circumstances, these interviews are all subject to the same basic rules, rules that the interviewers are probably familiar with, though not necessarily conscious of, because they have gone through the same procedure so many times. If they have had no training in interviewing they have probably learnt through bitter experience that unless they get it right, the results obtained from the interview are rather less than useful and can even be downright dangerous.

Managers are actually conducting interviews whenever a more junior member of staff comes in for advice or help in a work or private matter, when they go to visit a branch office to find out how business is or to the factory to inquire why there is a delay in filling orders. It might even be said that when they are chatting to a salesman about some new and complicated electronic gadgetry, finding out how it works and whether or not it will improve efficiency, they are conducting an interview.

However, most managers have no training in interviewing and, to make matters worse, many fear it. What they do not realize is that they have probably gained considerable experience in basic interviewing skills through their daily contact with staff and the outside world; all they need is a plan, a system to help them sort out the muddle of impressions usually gained from their failures.

That is what my interview plan is all about!

When you come to think of it, interviewing is a very artificial means of communication. Here you have two people, who have in many cases never set eyes on each other before, engaged in talking about subjects that may be of great importance and intimacy to one or both of them. They pretend they are meeting each other as equals, though they are not, because one, the interviewer, is usually in a much more powerful position than the interviewee. Although they both pretend to be at ease and to treat each other with a certain amount of informality, at least one of the participants is liable to be nervous and anxious. The way they sit, the way they talk, even the things that are said are designed not only to impart information but also, in some interviews, to impress the other participant.

There is also a pretence at being engaged in a free exchange of ideas, but it is nothing of the kind. The exchange, such as it is, is conducted according to fairly formal, though unspoken, rules under the control of the interviewer, who decides when to start it and when to end it and directs its course.

Despite its artificiality, the interview, when properly conducted, can be one of the best ways to obtain information for a great many purposes. In the hands of a skilled practitioner it is like a sharp knife that can cut away all the fat of irrelevant detail to get to the meat of the subject.

In job selection, for instance, a skilled interviewer can arrive at results about the suitability of a candidate as accurately as a whole swathe of intelligence and aptitude tests. In the day-to-day running of an office, a manager who knows how to interview and does so regularly is more likely to have good relations with his staff than the manager who depends on rules and regulations.

Interviews can do a great deal more. The manager who has to settle complaints, heal hurt pride or enforce discipline will find that asking questions and listening to replies are still among the best and most natural methods by which to resolve awkward staff problems, as any psychiatrist will confirm.

It should be mentioned that the interview can also create good public relations for a company. The applicant who comes for a job, the salesman for a sale or the customer for a refund may end up with none of these things but still come away with a very favourable impression of the company, because, in the interviews that took place, the managers asked the right questions and listened properly to the answers, giving the impression that they and, by association, the company are responsive and understanding.

Nevertheless, it must be said that a number of experts, particularly in the field of employment selection, have pointed out that in the hands of a clumsy interviewer the interview is more like a heavy blunt instrument than a sharp knife and does more harm than good. They contend that too much is at stake for both interviewer and applicant and that, as a result of the tension that exists between them, they are both likely to make wrong choices, the interviewer taking on someone unsuited for the job or rejecting someone well suited to it, the applicant either taking on an unsuitable job or rejecting a position for which he is well suited.

Selections based on impressions gained at an interview are regarded as highly suspect because they are so subjective, and it is almost impossible to make valid predictions about how someone is likely to develop in a job from one or two meetings across a table. Both are putting on a show, so they do not see each other as they really are, which may lead to the 'halo effect', whereby the interviewer decides positively in favour of all the candidate's qualities on the basis of one or two.

Whether or not the interview is always the best method or not, managers in every kind of business, as well as doctors, lawyers, social workers, researchers and the host of other professionals whose work depends to a smaller or larger extent upon gathering information will continue to go on using it despite its disadvantages, because it is still the easiest and most flexible form of communication between one human being and another upon which to base viable decisions.

DEFINITION

○○○

Many writers have described the interview as a conversation with a purpose. Interviews and conversations certainly do resemble each other – they take place between a minimum of two people, they are based on questions and answers and information passes from one to the other, but, if you analyse them, you'll see that the resemblance is superficial. Interviews should sound like conversations and the best do, with the participants getting on well together and the information flowing to and fro, but the dynamics of both differ in many important respects.

Conversations are usually unplanned and spontaneous, while interviews tend to be pre-arranged.

Conversations are unstructured, with questions and answers flowing back and forth in no particular order. Interviews are, or should be, planned, and one person, the interviewer, asks the questions, which the other, the interviewee, answers.

Conversations are not about any special topic but roam freely over a number of subjects; interviews deal with one main topic, be it a job, a complaint, information, though it may require the examination of a number of smaller topics to reach the larger.

Conversations occur between two people on an equal footing with no one controlling the flow of information back and forth. Interviews are usually conducted between two people of unequal standing and power and they should be in the control of the interviewer.

Conversations are supposed to be fun for both participants; interviews have a serious purpose and there is usually too much at stake, at least for one of the parties.

Some commentators have also likened the interview to a stage production, and here, too, there are superficial resemblances.

As in a play, the two participants are acting out roles; the interviewee plays the main role, while the interviewer is partly straight man, partly scriptwriter and partly stage manager and prompt.

As in a play, not much is left to chance. The performance is controlled, though there are climaxes and anticlimaxes, moments of tension and moments of ease. There is laughter and, unfortunately, there may also be tears.

The questions the interviewer asks are the script.

The room in which the interview is held is the stage and it is often deliberately designed, either to make the interviewee feel relaxed or to put the interviewee under pressure.

However, the important point to remember is that if the interview does resemble a play, it is a very private performance, with the actors also being the audience. One should not think of the interview as a chat show on television with an audience of millions. That kind of interviewing is part of show business, the purpose of which is to entertain, not to obtain information, and as such it has no place in the office. It must be mentioned, though, that some of the best chat-show hosts are able to convey, both to the audience and to their guests, that all-important sense of ease that produces the maximum of rapport.

So, what do we mean by an interview? According to *The Oxford English Dictionary*, an interview is a meeting of persons face to face for a particular purpose in which one asks the questions that the other is expected to answer.

If we analyse this definition closely, we see that certain vital elements about the interview emerge. The interview is:

- a meeting deliberately set up
- between two (or more) parties
- for a purpose
- in the control of one party
- who asks the questions
- the other party answers.

Each of these elements must be present for the interview to work and each has very important consequences, which will be examined in detail later on, but for the moment it is important to note two points.

Firstly, the meeting is deliberate, not a mere chance encounter. This is obvious in the majority of interviews, which are arranged in advance, but even when the meeting is apparently spontaneous, a closer examination often reveals this not to be so. Employees who 'by chance' bump into their superior in the corridor and 'by chance' mention some grievance that has been weighing on their mind and that they need to talk about have probably spent hours, if not days, wondering how to engineer the meeting. The good manager will recognize the ruse and will, preferably, arrange to discuss the matter in greater detail at a more convenient time and place to allow time to prepare.

Secondly, interviews are always held for a purpose, and the interviewer must be conscious of this fact before and during the interview. Much of the ability to control the interview depends upon it. Managers who go into an interview not knowing exactly why it has been arranged and do not make any effort to find out the reason are asking for trouble. What they certainly will not get, unless they are very lucky, is the kind of detailed information needed to make the right decisions.

There are two main forms of interview: structured and unstructured.

Structured

Here all the questions and all possible answers have been carefully formulated prior to the interview, and in the course of the interview the interviewer does not depart from those questions. In answering them, the interviewee is restricted to a choice of answers and cannot deviate from them.

In some instances, interviewees are shown a card upon which the choice of answers is stated and all they have to do is pick the answer that most closely fits the situation. Neither participant can develop the subject beyond its given limits. Market research and opinion poll interviews are mainly of this kind, though increasingly the structured interview is being used in employment selection and also in diagnostic interviewing in medicine.

Unstructured

Although the interviewer has defined the objectives to be achieved in the interview and has probably worked out the main questions beforehand, there is far more freedom in this type of interview to alter the questions or the order in which they are asked. The interviewer can also develop themes suggested by the interviewee's answers. The interviewee is encouraged throughout to do most of the talking, with the interviewer guiding, probing and summing up as the interview demands.

Most management, research and decision-making interviewing falls into this category, and it is this form of interviewing that is dealt with in this book.

PARTICIPANTS

ooo

Having established what we mean by an interview, let us look at the two participants.

I. THE INTERVIEWER

The ideal interviewer is not the ideal salesperson. The two are opposites of each other. The salesperson is a go-getter, a domineering individual intent on persuasion. The ideal interviewer is intent not on talking but on encouraging others to talk.

A group of students studying interview techniques was asked to identify the main qualities of the ideal interviewer and they came up with the following list: serious-minded; self-disciplined; self-controlled; free of prejudices, tolerant and understanding of other people; possessing a high degree of empathy with others; mental poise so that they can react quickly to changes of direction in the interview; physical poise and presence so that the interviewer appears at ease in all situations; a clear speaking voice; and the ability to listen with understanding.

No one, of course, is perfect; these are the attributes of the ideal interviewer. Nonetheless, it is useful to look at them in more detail to see how they apply to the ordinary manager trying to cope with the problem of interviewing on a day-to-day basis.

Serious-minded interviewers go into an interview determined to get the most out of it and do not regard it as an annoying interruption in their busy day. However, it does not mean they are solemn and lacking in humour, because, used appropriately, humour can be a marvellous way to help an interviewee feel at ease and to aid the interviewer through sticky patches that sometimes arise.

Self-disciplined interviewers go into an interview properly prepared. When job applicants were asked in a survey which interviewers they most liked, most chose those who had read the job specification as well as their application forms so that they were ready with the right questions and did not waste time going over ground already covered by the application forms. To read the forms and plan the questions that should be answered in advance requires self-discipline. It is much easier to leave things to chance and hope that the interviewee will provide all the necessary answers without too much effort.

Self-controlled interviewers remain calm no matter what the circumstances. They do not lose their temper or argue with the interviewee, nor do they try to belittle the interviewee or insult his or her intelligence. They are confident of themselves and convey to the interviewee that they are in charge of the interview, without resorting to power games. The interviewer who has self-control also has control of the interview.

In the multi-ethnic society in which we live, unprejudiced interviewers are no longer an asset to an organization but a necessity. They are able to make mature, valid assessments about the qualities of those they interview because they do not judge others merely by their skin colour or their accent. Prejudices extend beyond race and class to the way other people live. The manager who disapproves of women working, for example, is not likely to listen with understanding to a female member of staff whose work is suffering because of family difficulties.

The wider the range of life experiences interviewers have, the more likely they are to have an open mind about the lifestyles of others and the less likely they are to be shocked. No one, however, is totally without prejudice; only the best interviewers have sufficient insight to know the extent of their prejudices and to keep them in check, not only when conducting interviews but also in assessing the results.

Ideally, the interviewer should possess a high degree of empathy. Empathy is the ability to put yourself in an interviewee's place and to understand his or her problem. Sympathy, on the other hand, is becoming absorbed in the problem itself. There is a vital difference between empathy and sympathy, which anyone who has done some interviewing, particularly of a kind that involves the interviewee's emotions or state of mind, knows full well.

The difference between the two may amount to no more than a gesture. If any member of your staff comes to you, asking for your help, you will, in the first instance, find out what the problem is. By asking the right kind of questions and listening with understanding to the replies, you will help him or her to come to some decisions about the problem under discussion. This is empathy. If, when listening, you start to interrupt with expressions like 'I know just how you feel!', you have crossed the fine line between empathy and sympathy. Now your own emotions are engaged and you have thus lost your detachment and been drawn into the problem. By showing sympathy, you are making it more difficult for the interviewee to articulate the problem and, for your pains, you earn hostility and resentment for interfering.

Like it or not, the interviewer has to be tough-minded. Those who are too easily drawn into other people's lives or who can be easily manipulated by others do not make good interviewers, until, that is, they develop the necessary strength of purpose and objectivity to distance themselves from the interviewee. Fortunately, the more interviewing you do, the easier it becomes to do this.

Empathy and the ability to listen usually go together. The interviewer who has empathy is also likely to be the one who can listen with understanding. Such interviewers will let the interviewee do most of the talking, which is as it should be.

Interviewers are, however, human. They too may have personality problems. Here are some of the difficulties that can get in the way of the good interview:

- timidity
- tendency to panic
- being easily led (or, rather, misled)
- ignorance of the subject of the interview
- lack of organization

- inability to select what is relevant
- lack of foresight.

Summed up, the two most common blocks are fear and unpreparedness. I shall be discussing preparation in much greater detail further on. Fear is a more difficult problem to deal with, but it is much alleviated by practice. On the other hand, it is exacerbated by lack of preparation. The better prepared you are for an interview, therefore, the less you have to fear.

Let's now look at motivations or, in simpler terms, why bother to interview? The most obvious motivation is that interviewing is part of your job; but there are others that may operate in your favour to make you a better interviewer, including:

- interest in the interviewee's career, as in the evaluation or assessment interview
- interest in the outcome of the interview, as in the counselling or problem-solving interview
- viewing it as a challenge, as in the grievance or disciplinary interview
- a desire to help others, as in any of the above
- curiosity about other people, as in all types of interviewing. A genuine curiosity about what makes other human beings tick is a necessary requirement of good interviewing. It is not that you want to pry into the interviewee's private life – in fact, you are specifically warned against it; but your interest in the interviewee, which you show in various ways, is what helps make the interview, of whatever kind, a success.

2. THE INTERVIEWEE

As with the interviewer, so with the interviewee: fear is the main block that may prevent the establishing of mutual trust and rapport so necessary for the successful outcome of the interview. The interviewee's fear may take several forms:

- fear of the interviewer
- fear of the result of the interview
- fear of appearing foolish or ignorant.

In addition, a suspicion or dislike of the interviewer based on previous bad experience militates against the happy outcome of an interview.

None of this should be surprising when you think of what an interview is. To spend time with a person you have either never met before or know only in the restricted surroundings of an office or factory and answer questions, sometimes of a very personal nature, is most unnatural. Interviewers who fail to recognize this and expect interviewees to respond in a full, confident manner right from the outset without any encouragement are bound to be disappointed. Good interviewers are prepared for awkwardness, embarrassment and nervousness and consequently are in a much better position to deal with these problems, should they arise.

Some interviews, such as disciplinary and grievance interviews, are by their very nature difficult, because the interviewee is going to be anxious and also possibly resentful and aggressive. In such circumstances, the desired easy flow of information from interviewee to interviewer is going to be severely blocked by these strong emotions. Again, the good interviewer should be aware of the dangers and be prepared for them.

However, to counterbalance the blocks there are some all-important motivations, which help to make the interviewer's life easier. The following come immediately to mind:

- a strong desire for a successful outcome
- a wish to please the interviewer
- an emotional release, a way of unburdening
- a desire to make a point or confirm an opinion
- a chance to right a wrong.

For example, suppose a manager has noticed that the work of a member of staff has deteriorated and is concerned that the employee may be bothered by a problem, either at work or at home; the employee is invited into the office for a 'talk'. (Note: the word 'talk' is used rather than 'interview', because some people are terrified by the idea of an interview, which reminds them of nasty confrontations with people like head teachers!)

The manager has set aside some time to give undivided attention to the employee and has prepared a few pertinent questions, helped by knowing the purpose of the interview. The manager knows the interviewee is probably going to be reluctant to talk and wants to encourage and reassure the employee by pointing out how it can help. The opening remarks, therefore, are geared to that purpose.

INTERVIEWER: I get the impression that your mind's not been on your work lately and I'd like to give you the opportunity of saying if this is so or not. If it is, perhaps you could tell me what it is that's troubling you and I may be able to help.

INTERVIEWEE: I'd rather not talk about it.

INTERVIEWER: If you're worried about it going out of this office, don't be. Anything private you tell me will be kept in confidence.

By emphasizing a relevant motivation (the chance to talk about a problem that is interfering with the employee's work), and by allaying a fear (that intimate, private details will be spread around the office), the manager may persuade the employee to discuss the matter. If the employee should continue to refuse, the manager will probe to find out why and by the further skilful employment of any of the above motivations change the 'No' into a 'Yes'.

Part 2: The Interview Plan

STAGE 1: DEFINING THE PURPOSE

ooo

Every interview has a purpose and the more clearly you define that purpose:

- the better you will be prepared for the interview
- the easier it will be for you to formulate and order your questions
- the more flexible you will be in meeting problems if they should arise in the interview
- the more accurate and coherent will be your evaluation when the interview is finished.

Therefore, as soon as you know an interview is to take place:

- decide on the purpose
- write it down, if possible
- remember it throughout the interview.

The following are some examples of what I mean by defining the purpose.

A job selection interview: to draw out as much relevant information from and gain sufficient impressions about the candidates to allow the interviewer to make an accurate assessment of their suitability for the job as defined by the job specification (or the job advertisement).

An appraisal interview: to learn about the employees' views and attitudes to the job and how they are progressing (or not), to help them to rate themselves against the job's requirements; and to motivate and encourage them.

An information-gathering interview: to obtain as much relevant information from the interviewee about the subject, so as to be able to make a proper selection of the data for the use to which the interviewer intends to put it.

A problem-solving interview: to help the interviewees to articulate the problem in order to be able to come to some rational understanding of it, on the basis of which they can make appropriate and constructive decisions to solve it.

A disciplinary interview: to confirm the facts of the interviewees' misconduct and then to help them towards an understanding of the nature of the misconduct and how they must improve their performance in the future. (Its aim is thus not to punish but to restore a balance.)

Note: the initiative to hold the interview does not always lie with the interviewer. In problem-solving interviews, for example, it may be initiated by the interviewee. Nonetheless, it is *always* the responsibility of the interviewer to establish a purpose for and an objective to be reached by the interview. So the early stages of the interview will be taken up by the kind of probing questions that will do just that. Once the purpose has been established and accepted by both the interviewer and interviewee, the interview may proceed in the usual way.

Points to Remember

1. Every interview has a purpose.

2. That purpose must be clear in your mind before the interview starts.

3. It must be kept in your mind throughout the interview.

4. When assessing the interview, you have to compare the purpose you had in mind with the results to see if the interview met the purpose.

Above the specific purpose of the particular interview, however, there is a larger, more general purpose, which applies to *all* interviews: *make the interview a rewarding experience for both of you.*

At first glance this goal may seem a tall order, suited more to the realms of fantasy than to the hurly-burly of a busy office; but in fact it is not so difficult to achieve and is vital to the conduct and successful outcome of an interview that you have such an aim. In time and with practice it will be there without you even having to think about it.

What does it mean?

It means that both you and the interviewee should get something out of the interview above and beyond the mere mechanics of asking and answering questions, because, if that is all there is to it, neither of you will feel that it has accomplished very much. Worse still, you will feel that the information was not the best that could be obtained in the time available.

It means that, although you are meeting another human being in circumstances that for both of you, and more particularly the interviewee, are strange and daunting, you have managed to create an agreeable and reassuring atmosphere in which the flow of information is encouraged to take place unimpeded.

It means that whatever the outcome, the interviewee is never left to feel undervalued as a human being, but rather that it has been a valuable experience from which something useful and positive has been gained, if only the opportunity to talk to an interested, well-prepared and understanding listener. In job selection interviews, for example, it is important, both from the point of view of the interviewees and of the organization you represent, that the interviewees feel they have had a fair hearing and been given a fair opportunity for the job.

It means that in some way, large or small, both of you have been changed by the interview. You both know more about each other than you did before the interview and understand more about each other and about yourselves. This is the essence and goal of the psychotherapeutic interview in which, guided by the therapist's questioning, the client reaches an awareness of the sources of his or her problems and as a result of such awareness is helped to resolve them. The aim of all interviewing should be a greater awareness through which comes better understanding.

It means, in short, that like most things of any value in life, the more involved you are and the more you put into the interview, the more you will get out of it.

How you do this and how you make interviewing rewarding is the underlying theme of the rest of this book.

So, read on!

Recognize this scene? A young school-leaver is coming to see you about the job as an office junior. You knew about this well in advance because she sent you a curriculum vitae (c.v.) and the appointment was clearly marked in your diary, but on the morning of the interview other things have cropped up. Anyway, you hate interviewing because you never seem to know the best questions to ask.

She arrives on time, a little nervous but keen to get the job, so she is ready for all you can throw at her. You, on the other hand, are harassed, running late, your phone is ringing, your office untidy and you've not had a moment to study her c.v.

The interview begins, but after you have put a few preliminary questions to her about her school career, because that's all you can think of on the spur of the moment, you have a complete mental block and can't even remember what an office junior is supposed to do, except keep the coffee percolator going. After this there are gaps of increasing length between her answers and your questions.

Half an hour later you both stagger out, relieved that it is over, you without a clue whether or not she is any good for the job, she totally put off both you and the idea of working for such a muddle-headed, disorganized boss. Hardly a rewarding and enjoyable experience for either of you, the interview, as a means of selecting the right person for the job, was a complete waste of time.

The story has several morals. Firstly, good interviews of whatever nature depend, to a large extent, on how clearly the objectives of the interview are defined and how accurately the main questions reflect these objectives. Put more simply, you should know what you wish to achieve from the interview, because you cannot depend on your interviewee to show you the way.

Secondly, it pays to take care and time defining your objectives before you start and then frame your questions accordingly. Write down what those objectives are so that you have them in front of you when formulating your questions.

Thirdly, in order to prepare for the interview, you will usually have to do some background reading or research. In the example above, a few minutes with the applicant's c.v. might have made all the difference to the outcome of the interview, because then at least you would have been in a position to pose some useful questions instead of spending time during the interview thinking of things to say.

If, for instance, your interviewee has fixed an appointment to see you about a complaint, you ought, if you don't know him well, to acquaint yourself with who he is, how long he has been with the company, his record and the quality of his work. It is not a good idea to know too many details about the complaint itself, otherwise you may be tempted to prejudge the issue and use the interview as an opportunity to lecture him. Aim to know enough background to be able to put useful and intelligent questions, but not so much that there is no room for developing or opening up new areas of interest in the course of the interview.

Finally, whatever happens, make sure you know *something*. There are few things more likely to make an interviewee irritable and unresponsive than to be faced by an interviewer who has done no preparation, either with regard to the interviewee or the subject-matter of the interview.

Do not be like the cub reporter from a local newspaper who came to interview me about a book I had recently published. His opening words are etched on my memory as how not to start an interview. 'I'm sorry,' he apologized, 'but I don't know who you are or anything about your book, but my editor sent me to ask you a few questions.' That interview, as you can imagine, was a waste of time for both of us.

STAGE 2: SETTING UP THE INTERVIEW

ooo

At this point it is worth remembering that *the overall purpose of an interview is to make the experience a rewarding one for both participants, in which the fullest possible information has been obtained so that decisions can be made and action taken on the basis of that information.*

In order to achieve this it is vital that the interview takes place in surroundings to suit both you and the interviewee. This, of course, is not always possible. Interviews cannot always be arranged in advance to give you time to set them up properly and the only available venue may not be the most suitable; but you should, nonetheless, make every effort to create the best setting for the interview. Much depends upon it, and the responsibility for this is yours and yours alone.

The rules about surroundings are simple:

- everything that concentrates the interviewee's attention is good
- everything that distracts the interviewee's attention is bad.

Distraction is the enemy of good interviewing. If interviewees are, for one reason or another, unable to give their full and undivided attention to what you are asking and to what they are answering, then the result is a failure or only a partial success. And since, very often, interviews are one-off meetings, you never get another chance to correct matters with the same interviewee.

What, then, is the ideal setting? It is the one that best suits the interviewees, i.e. one that will allow them to concentrate on your questions so that they may give their answers, free of distractions. The setting consists of the room, the seating arrangement and the ambience.

I. THE ROOM

The rule is that everything that distracts the interviewee's attention is bad, and everything that concentrates it is good, so the room should be seen, as far as possible, from the viewpoint of the interviewee. As the interviewee is probably somewhat anxious or at least self-conscious, the room should be as neutrally pleasant as possible.

Rooms on which the character of the interviewer is too firmly stamped can be very daunting as the interviewee feels like an intruder who has unwittingly stumbled into someone else's private space. Rooms filled with bric-à-brac, crammed with eye-catching paintings and posters or packed to the ceiling with ostentatious ornaments are going to make the interviewer's task doubly difficult because the interviewee's attention is continually drawn away from the main purpose of the meeting.

On the other hand, rooms like station waiting-rooms, cold and uninviting, and rooms in which no care or thought is given to the comfort of visitors may not positively distract the interviewees – there's nothing for them to look at, but they certainly will not make them feel at ease and eager to give of their best.

It pays, therefore, to look at the room in which you customarily interview to see if you can improve it in any way, remembering to try to see it as the interviewee would see it. Perhaps the products you have stacked up in the corner are selling the company just a bit too hard. Perhaps those advertising posters around the walls are too spectacular; and what about those executive toys you've been collecting on your desk? – wiry things that move with the breeze, making clicking noises, which it is OK to amuse your colleagues with but are the death of the interview. If you happen to be the macho type and like to decorate your office with calendars showing naked women disporting themselves against the background of tropical beaches, you are going to embarrass and put off any female interviewee who is unfortunate enough to enter your office.

Drab rooms without any decoration or ornamentation can also have the wrong effect on the interview. If you do not want to turn an interview into an interrogation, choose a place in which you both can feel comfortable and relaxed, but not too comfortable – you do not want your interviewee falling asleep! A vase of fresh flowers, for instance, so long as neither the vase nor the flower arrangement is eye-catching, can be a pleasant and undistracting background. Paintings and posters, especially if they are relevant to your organization's business, can become useful talking points to break the ice at the start of the interview – and then be immediately forgotten. Company products, such as a publisher's latest books, can tell the interviewee more about the company than you can.

One point often overlooked by interviewers is the lighting. Here too a little forethought can make life easier for both of you. Avoid having glare and lights shining into your own or the interviewee's eyes. A fact known to interrogators all over the world is that bright lights shining into suspects' eyes cause confusion and disorientation, so that it is possible to plant information into their brains to make them confess to crimes they did not commit. Similarly, though on a less sinister scale, a bright office lamp shining directly into interviewees' eyes can result in them telling you things you are not required to know or giving you answers that they think you want to hear. Either way, the information has not been freely and willingly given.

If, therefore, you are sitting with your back to a window and you place the interviewees in a chair facing the window, when the sun shines they will have to squint to see you properly, and even then your face will be shaded and your eyes obscured. As we shall see later, it is vital that the interviewees can see your eyes.

Ideally, the lighting should be bright enough so that you can both clearly see each other and each other's eyes but subdued enough to produce a warm, friendly and relaxed atmosphere.

It is a thoughtful gesture to provide stands or hooks, either in the office itself or just outside, on which interviewees can put their coats, hats and umbrellas. If the interviewees come in from a heavy storm and are interviewed clutching a soaking raincoat and hat, propping up a dripping umbrella and in terror of ruining the interviewer's carpet, they are not going to make the most of their answers.

2. THE SEATING ARRANGEMENT

The seating arrangement is one of the first things the interviewee sees on entering your office, and the messages it should give are:

- I'm approachable
- I have time to listen to you
- I am interested to hear what you have to say.

What the seating arrangement should *not* say is:

- I am more important than you
- you're a nuisance
- I haven't time to spare.

The Desk

Is your desk really necessary for the interview? Yes, if you feel you need to protect yourself from the interviewee; no, if you don't.

A desk between you and the interviewee signals your inaccessibility or even your fear of the interviewee. It is somewhere safe for you to hide behind. A job applicant faced with a desk furnished with a bank of telephones, stacks of files and reams of computer print-out will quickly get the point that you are very busy and important and that every second of your time is precious – not, I would suggest, the kind of impression diffident interviewees need. It will not reassure them or encourage them to reveal useful information about themselves that may determine who is suitable for the post.

Even in the most difficult interviews, such as those involving discipline or dismissal, you and the interviewee are, or ought to be, on the same side, literally as well as figuratively. You, as an individual, may dislike the interviewee and feel strongly about the reasons for the dismissal, but you are not enemies. As a manager, you still must protect your company's good name, your own reputation as being fair minded and the interviewee's self-respect.

In other kinds of interviewing, there should be no reason for animosity between you and the interviewee, and there should therefore be no reason for a desk to separate the two of you. Of course, that is precisely what a desk does – it separates and protects.

You may be the interviewee's superior in the company hierarchy and you may have far more power, but the interview is not the time nor the place to remind any interviewee of this, particularly if he or she is coming to see you for your understanding and help.

So, unless your office is so small that you cannot sit anywhere but at your desk, come out from behind it and meet your interviewee as an equal. If you want to take notes, you can place a small table by your side or keep a notebook on your lap where you can jot down what you have to.

The Chairs

As with desks, the message your chairs should give the interviewees is that, no matter how important a position you occupy in the company or in the world at large, you regard them as human beings, who, as such, are entitled to the same respect you would expect from them. Your chairs should reflect this warm, positive attitude. Avoid the embarrassment of playing musical chairs, where you both make for the most comfortable chair, leaving the less comfortable for the other. Interviews should not be places for favourites and it should not matter which of the two chairs you sit in.

Chairs should be comfortable but not so luxurious that the interviewee (or interviewer) will want to fall asleep in them and of the same kind and the same height. The interviewer's should not be a few inches higher and upholstered in leather, while the interviewee's is made of aluminium tubing and canvas. They should be placed at approximately 60° to each other and about four feet apart. If the chairs are any closer than three feet, the distance will be too informal and intimate; further apart – say, more than five feet – and it will be too formal and remote. (For more information on this, see Body Language and Eye Contact in Stage 4: Managing the Interview.)

Other Furniture

A small coffee-table placed between and slightly in front of the participants has its uses as a base for making notes, keeping relevant documents at hand or simply as a place on which to put cups of coffee or tea if they are being served. Interviewees should not be expected to balance a cup and saucer on their laps or burn their fingers trying to hold a polystyrene cup of hot liquid from the coffee dispenser. The table will give them a place to dispose of the container when they are finished with it.

If a tape recorder is being used to record the interview, it too can be placed on the table.

3.   THE AMBIENCE

Remember: whatever concentrates the interviewee's mind is good; whatever distracts it is bad. The following distract:

- glare
- noise
- persistent interruptions.

We have looked at the importance of lighting and avoiding glare; the other two need a little more explanation.

Noise, from whatever source, will impede the free flow of information between you and the interviewees. You may be used to the hum of the air-conditioning or the cars revving up outside your window and not even notice them, but the interviewees are probably being exposed to it for the first time and may not even hear your questions properly. Reluctant to ask you to shut the window or too embarrassed to keep asking you to repeat your questions, in the end they will answer what they think you asked. You probably won't understand the answers and will think they are being deliberately obstructive or eccentric. As a result, a chasm of misunderstanding will have been created between the two of you, too wide to be bridged.

Interruptions, such as telephone calls or other members of staff coming in to see you, will also severely block the flow of information. Every time the telephone rings or there is a knock on the door, whoever is speaking has to stop and start again when the interruption has ceased, by which time the line of thought may have been forgotten. It should not be too difficult to discourage callers or to have an 'Engaged' sign on the door; the gesture would be greatly appreciated, because it would show the interviewee how seriously you are taking the interview. Many managers do neither, preferring, albeit unconsciously, to impress the interviewee with how busy and important they are.

To smoke or not to smoke? There can be no firm ruling on this; everything depends on the interviewer's attitude towards smoking. If both you and the interviewee are smokers, then presumably you will not object to the interviewee smoking, in which case you ought to provide ashtrays. The presence of an ashtray on the table in front of the interviewee is an invitation to smoke. If, however, you disapprove of smoking, you may prefer not to permit the interviewee to smoke. An interviewee who lights up without being given the go-ahead is displaying bad manners and should be asked to put out the cigarette. There is no reason for you to suffer in silence.

To sum up: as far as it is within your power to arrange it, the setting should encourage interviewees to relax but at the same time be alert to your questions and to the answers they give you. The room should be free of noise and any other distractions, the lighting clear but subdued, and there should be no interruptions. Chairs of the same height and type should be placed about four feet away from each other at an angle of approximately 60°, with, if desired, a low coffee-table conveniently in front of both of you. You should provide a place for interviewees to hang their coats, hats and umbrellas. If you smoke or permit smoking, you should supply ashtrays.

Even if, due to lack of facilities and space, it is not possible to provide all the above, it is worth trying to achieve an approximation. Your interviews will be easier to conduct and better for it.

STAGE 3: MEETING AND GREETING

ooo

The relationship between interviewer and interviewee is essentially artificial and, accordingly, fraught with problems, and it is therefore vital that a good, trusting relationship is created between you and the interviewee and maintained throughout the interview.

The interview is in your hands, so the responsibility for establishing a rapport with your interviewee is yours. Rapport is not a friendship, nor a kinship of like minds. It is established when both sides communicate clearly, freely, openly and with due seriousness. It evolves from an understanding between you that you are conducting the interview because you have information to obtain and the interviewee has information to give, upon which decisions of one kind or another will be based; and how effective or otherwise those decisions are depends to a large extent on how effective the rapport is.

This does not mean there is no place for friendliness. On the contrary, it is very important that you are seen to be willing to listen, because the interviewee will take the cue from you. If you come out to greet interviewees with a smile on your face and a hand held out in a friendly manner, they are going to respond in like fashion, no matter how nervous and anxious, resentful or angry they may be feeling. It is very difficult not to. If you meet the interviewee with a stern frown, a clipped greeting or a silent, impatient gesture towards a chair, the interviewee is going to find it impossible to act in a friendly way towards you.

You do not need an interviewee's friendship; nor do you have to go begging, cap in hand, for co-operation. The opinion that the interviewees will form of you, whether of open-mindedness and a willingness to listen or of the opposite, will probably stay with them right till the end of the interview, and that opinion depends to a large extent on their first impressions of you.

If, therefore, from the first contact you make with the interviewee you establish a degree of trust between you, it will make your task very much easier. Any problems that may arise during the course of the interview can be dealt with without undue stress and disruption.

How, then, do you establish this initial rapport? There are a number of simple rules.

Where an interview has been arranged in advance, try to go yourself to collect the interviewee from the waiting-room (which should also be as undaunting and as pleasant a room as possible).

Some interviewers, I know, will balk at this, especially if the interviewee is a young college graduate or, worse, a school-leaver! 'It's demeaning,' they'll say (or think). 'How can I establish my authority and the dignity of my position if I go myself to welcome a young school-leaver? What are secretaries for?'

If that is your reaction, think of it in a self-interested way. The purpose of interviewing is to get the best information possible so that you can make the right decisions – decisions that may, after all, affect your own future position. If you treat a job interview as no more than a necessary evil that has to be got over with as quickly as possible and from the start fail to establish rapport with the interviewee, you may choose an unsuitable applicant with horrendous results for your organization and, ultimately, yourself.

Interviewees are guaranteed to be put off if they have to go through ranks of unhelpful secretaries before reaching the Holy of Holies, if they are summoned by a buzzer or, worst of all, if they are confronted by an electronic system of red and green lights such as some executives use on their doors, presumably to show their authority. (I have seen how such systems adversely affect the very people with whom the manager wishes and needs to retain good relationships. A former employer of mine installed a traffic light on his door and after a few weeks during which the staff stood outside his door and felt decidedly stupid, waiting for the red light to turn green, there was a revolt and we all took to marching into his office without even knocking. He soon got the point and removed the offending lights.)

If in the course of the day you are approached for an interview but are otherwise engaged at that moment, always make arrangements for the interview to take place as soon as possible.

Accessibility is the key to trustful relationships. The people you interview are those you may already be working with or those you may soon be working with on a close, day-to-day basis. You have nothing to lose and everything to gain by showing that you can be approached and that you are accessible.

Obviously, you cannot be available to everyone every minute of the day, otherwise you would not be able to get on with your own work, but people are not stupid. They realize this and will respect it, as long as, when they do come to you, you do not merely put them off with excuses about how busy you are but, there and then, arrange to see them at a time and place suitable to both.

If, as is usually the case in a job interview, the interviewee does not know you, always introduce yourself, giving your name and position in the organization.

INTERVIEWER: Hello. Thanks very much for coming. I am Jean Bloggs, the company secretary. I am interviewing all the applicants today, but, if your application is successful, you will be working for John Brown, the sales manager.

We all have names, and, even though we may choose not to address each other by them all the time, it is a friendly, welcoming gesture on your part to reveal yours to the interviewee. After all, you know the interviewee's name, or at least you should; why keep your own a secret? And even if it is emblazoned on your door, mentioning it when you introduce yourself is a good way of establishing rapport.

The interviewee is naturally curious about the person conducting the interview, and there is no harm in explaining what position you occupy in the organization, not in a haughty manner to establish another status symbol behind which to hide – like a big desk – or to show off your importance, but, as with your name, to come out from behind your anonymity and reveal yourself to the interviewee as another human being. There is a danger, of course, that interviewees may adjust their own answers to suit your status – if you occupy a very high position in the company they may act more humbly and deferentially than they really feel and give answers intended to impress you; but I think that is a risk worth taking.

Cultivate a line in friendly, non-threatening, non-committal chit-chat or ice-breakers to put the interviewee at ease.

Rushing straight into the interview can be a mistake, though not always. If both you and the interviewee know precisely what is wanted from the interview and you are on reasonably close working terms, it may not be necessary to engage in conversation that is not directly related to the subject of the interview. If, however, you are a complete stranger to the interviewee, who is feeling unsure and nervous, then the few moments before the interview proper begins can profitably be used by you to put the interviewee at ease by means of the ice-breakers.

What you choose to talk about is up to you, though it may depend to some extent on what you know about your interviewee. Some experts suggest, for example, that you chat about a common interest, if such interest exists, so that by the time you begin to ask your first question, the interviewee will be more relaxed and have a positive attitude towards you and the interview.

INTERVIEWER: I see you come from [*name place*]. I know it well/I drive through it often on my way to work. Ever go to the [*name pub/theatre/club/park, as appropriate*]?

Nervous interviewees may not respond immediately or at all, but it is worth persisting, because by your friendliness you will penetrate the wall of tension they have built around themselves.

The weather, travel and parking problems always make good, non-committal ice-breakers. Also, a brief discussion of the company and its products – especially if they are on view – is a good way to warm up and at the same time to lead the interviewee into the interview itself.

INTERVIEWER: I don't know if you noticed the posters in the passage on the way to my office, but they're the latest ads for our new model. What do you think of them?

You must feel at ease with the subject of the warm-up, otherwise it will become an exercise in fatuity as well as futility. You must not let it go on too long, because you will be deflected from the real purpose of the interview. In the warm-up it is also best to avoid:

- over-heartiness
- jokes, especially coarse ones
- personal remarks
- references to politics, religion, sex or race.

The last two need special mention. It is worth repeating that in the first few minutes (even seconds) of your meeting the interviewee, a relationship is set up, no matter how tenuously. Impressions, good or bad, are formed that may last throughout the interview. The friendly greeting, the firm, businesslike handshake and the few relaxing words will reassure interviewees that you are someone they can feel comfortable with and to whom they will want to give of their best. If you overdo the warmth of the greeting just a little, make the handshake a little too aggressive (more like a salesman's than a responsible executive's), throw out some ill-considered remark about the interviewee's appearance, you may have ruined the rest of the interview.

Suppose a male interviewer were to say to a female interviewee, 'Good to see you. Hey, I like that brooch/ring/pendant you're wearing. My mother used to wear one just like it.' The effect of such a casual, thoughtless remark, made in an attempt to put the interviewee at ease, could be that, while the interviewer has started to ask important questions on which she should be concentrating, the interviewee is either thinking 'Why did he say that? What's wrong with my brooch/ring/pendant? Is it really so old-fashioned?' or 'How dare he speak to me like that! What is it to him what brooch/ring/pendant I'm wearing?'

Or, again, in an effort to make conversation, the interviewer comments on the latest opinion polls showing the government is more or less popular than last week. As the interviewer does not know – and has no business to know – the interviewee's political views, the remark can adversely affect the atmosphere in which the interview will be conducted.

If the interviewee is of a different race or sex, the interviewer must be on guard against saying anything that can be interpreted as racist or sexist. The first example above could well fall into the latter category, since it could be argued that the male interviewer would not have made a similar observation about an item of male apparel.

STAGE 4: MANAGING THE INTERVIEW

ooo

This section contains an analysis of what happens during the interview itself, and, to help you follow the sequence of topics, they are listed below:

1. Warming Up

2. Controlling the Interview

3. The Questions You Ask

4. Question Strategy

5. Use of the Voice

6. Body Language

7. Eye Contact

8. The Art of Good Listening

9. Special Techniques

10. Problems Arising in the Interview.

1. WARMING UP

Think of the interview as a stage production: you are poised at that dramatic moment when the curtain rises and the performance is about to begin. You are director, prompt, stage manager and audience all rolled into one. You know what you want to happen and you know more or less how the show should turn out, but the spotlight is on the interviewees, who are the stars of the show, not you, and it is your task to get them to shine. You have done your best to put them at ease and now you are ready to let them speak the first lines.

Put more prosaically, you have introduced yourself and sat down with an interviewee, and the interview is about to begin. At this point numerous questions may be going through the interviewee's mind: Are you going to be fair? Will your questions touch on embarrassing points? Am I making a good impression? For the interviewees it is an anxious moment, because, like actors, they are about to make their first appearance and are uncertain how the audience is going to react.

A *little* nervousness is no bad thing, because it will help interviewees to give their best. If they are over-confident, they may, like actors who are too self-assured, trip over and fall flat on their faces. If interviewees are too anxious, they won't listen to your questions properly or give due thought to their answers, and this will impede the flow of information.

What you want is to make them feel they are in safe hands, i.e. that they are not under any threat, and that it is in their interests as well as yours to co-operate in establishing a good, workable rapport. This can best be achieved by putting the interviewees in the picture by briefly outlining the purpose of the interview and the subject areas you intend to cover.

Interviewees are like passengers in a car driven by a stranger. They may have a general idea of the destination, but if they do not know the route the driver is going to take, they are bound to be apprehensive. On the other hand, if the driver tells them where they are going and how they are going to get there, they can relax and not worry about reading the road signs. In the same way, by telling interviewees at the start of the interview the broad areas you are going to cover and the order in which you will do so, you will be put them at ease and at the same time give them a sense of purpose and direction. (This means, of course, doing some preparation in advance!) However, you should avoid getting bogged down in too much detail; all that is needed at this stage is an overview, which should be tailored to meet the requirements of the interview and the interviewee, as in the following examples.

For the job interview:

INTERVIEWER: Thank you for sending me your application form. We'll be looking at the areas covered by it in more detail, starting with your present job, then your previous work experience and finally I'd like to ask you some questions about your educational background. Then you'll have a chance to ask me any questions about the job or the company. OK? Then let's start with . . .

(Note: As we will discuss in more detail later, if in such a job interview the applicant is young and recently out of school or college, it is better to start with education. With an older or more senior applicant, to whom much of that is irrelevant and probably very boring, start with the most recent work experience and work backwards to education and other interests.)

For the appraisal interview:

INTERVIEWER: Thanks for sparing the time. I would like to find out how you're getting on in the new job so I'd like to talk about the pros and the cons – how much you're enjoying it and what problems, if any, you may be having. And, by the way, this is not meant as criticism. We're very pleased with the work you are doing.

For the counselling interview:

INTERVIEWER: I'm glad we're having this chance to talk. I understand you've a problem you want to discuss, so I suggest we take it step by step. First, let's hear what the problem is, then we can look at some possible solutions.

For the disciplinary interview:

INTERVIEWER: I have received a complaint about you from your supervisor/I have to say that I'm not satisfied with your work, so first I would like to tell you what the/my complaint is, then I'd like to hear what you have to say, then we'll try to find together a way of getting things back to normal/of improving things.

After preparing them in this way, your interviewees should be in the proper frame of mind to answer your first question.

2. CONTROLLING THE INTERVIEW

Back to first principles: the interview is a meeting deliberately set up between two parties for a purpose *in the control of one party*, who asks the questions, which the other party answers.

The interviewer controls the interview, not the interviewee. Friendliness and rapport are vital in order to achieve the purpose of the interview, but it must not be forgotten that time is money, and it is your task to get the most out of the interviewee in the given time. Interviews should therefore be conducted in an organized, businesslike way. As a general rule, the more time you have to fill, the more irrelevant questions you will find to fill it, so a discreet eye has to be kept on the clock to ensure that you manage the interview with the maximum of efficiency.

However, when I say 'control', I do not mean forcing the interviewees to go the way you want; I mean allowing them the space and freedom to express themselves under your guidance and direction. Without this guidance, the interview is likely to degenerate into chaos.

Controlling an interview is not only knowing how to motivate the interviewee to answer you fully and openly instead of with just a grunt, a nod or a single 'Yes' or 'No', it is also knowing how to stop the interviewee who develops a sudden attack of verbal diarrhoea.

Control does not mean dominating the interviewee, pushing faster than is appropriate or jumping impatiently from one subject to another. It means determining the right pace and giving the right kind of direction so that the time set aside for the interview is used to its fullest and neither you nor the interviewee feels that a moment has been wasted. In short, it is knowing how to conduct the interview so that you get from it the information you require in the time allotted to make the necessary decisions. Control is the single most important aspect of the interview and the one that probably gives more headaches to interviewers than any other.

First of all, remember to define your objectives in advance and plan your questions accordingly. You cannot predict the future. You do not know how your interviewee is going to behave, but if you define your objectives before the interview begins, you will be in a better position to exert control should the unexpected occur. You will recognize when the interviewee is veering away from the subject-matter, is attempting to take over or has lost the way. You will also know if you are covering the subject of the interview in full, penetrating those areas that need special attention, wasting your time by going off course, i.e. spending too much of it on unimportant matters and too little on important ones, or facing any of the other unexpected and unpredictable things that can go wrong in the interview and correcting them before it is too late.

How, then, do you achieve and maintain control? The main method by which the interviewer controls the interview is *by asking questions*, because, no matter how good the rapport between you and the interviewee, if your questions are inadequate, the interview will fail. As this is perhaps the most crucial aspect of interviewing, the questions you ask and the way you ask them are examined in detail below.

3.   THE QUESTIONS YOU ASK

Objectives

A good question is one that encourages the interviewee to answer freely and honestly. A bad question is one that inhibits the interviewee from answering freely or produces distorted information.

The questions you ask and the way you ask them should do two things:

1.   obtain the information you require
2.   motivate the interviewee to talk freely.

To achieve these two objectives, your questions should be:

- phrased positively
- framed in language the interviewee can understand
- restricted to the subject-matter of the interview
- limited to a single idea at a time
- serious and genuinely interested
- short and to the point.

Following from the above, here are some important do's and don'ts.

Do's

Keep the questions positively phrased. Start off positively and keep the interview on a positive note. Do not forget that you are in charge and the interviewee will look to you for a lead. You set the tone of the interview and if, by the way in which you phrase your questions you show that you have a positive, confident attitude towards the interviewee, the interviewee will respond in like manner. If, on the other hand, you are diffident and apologetic, the interviewee will either take charge – which means you will get nothing worthwhile out of it – or will be equally diffident and apologetic. The two of you will, in unspoken collusion, be carefully skirting around the important points, never really getting to grips with the subject-matter. Good, clear questions, positively framed, are the best indicator of an interviewer who knows what the interview is about and what objectives are being sought and who is in overall control of the interview.

INTERVIEWER: I would like you to tell me about . . .
   not
INTERVIEWER: I wonder if you would be willing to tell me about . . .

Treat the interviewee as an equal. That the interviewers and interviewees occupy different roles is no reason for the interviewers to consider themselves superior to the interviewee. Interviews should not be excuses to play power games. The interviewee will not respond readily to someone whose questions have been framed in a superior or arrogant manner.

INTERVIEWER: I see you qualified abroad. Would you say that your degree is as good as a British university degree?

Use language the interviewee can understand. Achieving mutual understanding should be an essential goal of the interviewer, because without it little the interviewee says will be of any value.

Lack of mutual understanding usually (though not always) results from the way the questions have been framed.

It could be that the interviewer, coming from a different class, cultural or educational background, uses a form of words that may be meaningless to the interviewee. The result is that the interviewee either will not answer or will give an inappropriate answer. 'What extra-curricular activities did you engage in?' may be all right for a university student but probably not for a school-leaver.

INTERVIEWER [*to junior*]: What ambivalences, if any, did you have to those in immediate authority over you?

(This was actually asked of a friend. Presumably the interviewer meant 'How did you get on with your previous boss?')

It may be that the interviewer tries too hard to be part of the interviewee's world. Questioning street-wise youngsters in their own language will produce a laugh or an answer that sends up your pretensions rather than the information you seek. The good interviewer whose task is to interview younger candidates will certainly try to keep up with the way they are thinking by reading teenage magazines and listening to radio programmes designed for the younger audience, but will not pretend to be something he or she is not. As slang changes so frequently, using outmoded words and phrases only serves to draw attention to the interviewer's ignorance.

The trick is to be yourself and use the idiom you feel most at home with, so long as it is one that can be plainly understood by the interviewee. In general, the simpler the language the better; if you are in any doubt as to whether the interviewee understood the question, repeat it in different ways to make sure.

Where the interviewee uses a word or phrase that you are not clear about, do not hesitate to ask for an explanation – rather that than risk getting the meaning wrong by guessing.

Ask only one question at a time. 'Are you, or have you ever been, a member of the Communist Party, and, if so, have you ever renounced your allegiance?' This is the kind of question that was asked during the McCarthy witch-hunts in America back in the

Fifties. Consisting of two different parts, each with two possible answers, its function, for which it was deliberately designed, was to confuse the interviewee, making it impossible to answer it properly without becoming trapped.

Without even being aware of doing so, it is easy for the interviewer to slip into multiple questions like the above, and the effect is the same: they confuse interviewees because they do not know which of the two (or more) questions to answer.

INTERVIEWER: At university, did you join any clubs and did you take an active part in them?

In this example, the possible answers may be mutually contradictory: 'I joined the debating club, but I took no active part in it.' If the candidate only answers 'Yes', the information received by the interviewer is distorted. Repeated frequently in an interview, multiple questions produce considerable distortion and should be avoided.

Sometimes, what seems like a multiple question is only a clarification and is therefore perfectly acceptable: 'How are you getting on in your new job? What are your feelings about it?' To make things clear, though, it is usually safer to ask only one question at a time.

Ask questions relevant to the subject-matter of the interview. If you know what the purpose of the interview is, you should have little trouble working out appropriate questions to ask and keeping the interviewee on track. On the other hand, if you go into the interview without sorting out what your objectives are, the chances are that you will be spending much of your time groping around in your mind for the next question while trying to listen to the answer of the last one. Eventually, you will lose your way and accomplished interviewees, who know more about interviewing than you do, will be able to lead you away from areas that for one reason or another they may prefer not to deal with.

Most interviewers have a limited time in which to conduct the interview, so time spent seeking information that can be obtained elsewhere, such as from the application form in a selection interview, is not only wasteful but is also irritating to the interviewee.

Asking questions for the sake of asking them may be construed by the interviewee as going beyond the bounds of legitimate 'need to know' into unacceptable 'want to know' questions out of idle curiosity. Your aim is to achieve the kind of relationship in which your interviewee feels relaxed enough to want to talk freely. What you don't want to is turn the interview into an interrogation where the interviewee feels that you are prying into private matters that are no concern of yours.

It is most tempting to ask such questions during the warm-up when you are trying to make your interviewee feel at ease and accordingly put questions that seem to you to be harmless in-quiries but to the interviewee may be unacceptably intrusive. Questions about the interviewee's appearance, for example, would fall under this heading. Irrelevant questions can crop up throughout the interview if you are not keeping track of what you are asking and what the interviewee is saying.

Questions relating to a prospective employee's religious or political beliefs are almost always irrelevant.

Knowing a job applicant's spare-time interests may be relevant, because they may reveal the interviewee's attitude to different aspects of life. A simple, direct question like 'What are your hobbies?' is perfectly acceptable, but 'How do you spend your evenings?' is not, since it is both ambiguous and out of place.

Ask non-sexist, non-racist questions. With the growing awareness of sexism and racism in society, a wide range of questions, which in the past were regarded as legitimate, have now, rightly, been seen for what they really are: demeaning and unjustifiable in-trusions into the rights of others. They should always now be avoided. To ask them may contravene the Sex Discrimination Act. If there is a reason for asking such a question, it should be put like this:

INTERVIEWER: You'll occasionally be asked to work till 7.00 p.m. Will you have any problems about that?
not
INTERVIEWER: As you have children, who will look after them if you are required sometimes to stay after 7.00 p.m.?

Recently, in a survey of women applying for teaching jobs, a number of blatantly sexist questions came to light. Single women were asked if they intended to get married and have a family. Married applicants were questioned about their children, if they were having more, if they had dependent relatives and who looked after them. Other especially offensive questions included 'Are you on the pill?' and 'How would an attractive woman like you cope with boys?' Another that should be avoided is 'How do you feel about working for a man/woman/younger person/a member of another race?'

There are, unfortunately, too many similar questions to be listed. As a general guide, when in doubt, leave out – it's safer – or ask yourself, 'If I were a woman or a member of an ethnic minority, how would I feel if I were asked that?'

Ask questions that encourage the interviewee to answer as fully as possible. Questions that require the interviewee to answer with a simple 'Yes' or 'No' inhibit the flow of the interview, and, if you ask them one after another, the interviewee is going to start to lose interest. Questions, therefore, should be framed so that interviewees are given ample opportunity to develop their answers to the full.

INTERVIEWER: Do you like the work you're doing at the moment?
INTERVIEWEE: No.
INTERVIEWER: Would you like a change?
INTERVIEWEE: Yes.

Interviews conducted like this are boring for both participants and little useful information about the interviewee's thoughts and feelings, which are often more important than facts, can be obtained from them.

Unfortunately, Yes/No questions seem to suggest themselves more easily to the interviewer than any other, which is yet another reason why it is vital that you prepare in advance at least half a dozen main questions to open up the interview and keep it going in a lively fashion. It must be said, however, that they have their uses, for instance when you wish to focus the interviewee's attention on a new subject.

INTERVIEWER: Let's now look at your other interests. Do you have any hobbies?
INTERVIEWEE: Yes.
INTERVIEWER: Good. Let's talk about them.

In general, such Yes/No questions should be avoided. If the above question were framed as 'What do you do in your spare time?', it would save time by allowing the interviewee to go straight into a more detailed description of his hobbies.

Ask simple, short, straightforward questions. It has been calculated that in the best interviews the interviewer speaks for only fifteen per cent of the time. If you have done your homework and prepared yourself properly, you should be able to put relevant and pertinent questions in a simple way, listen to the interviewee's replies and make sure that the interview continues in the direction you want it to take.

The simpler and shorter the questions, the easier it is for your interviewee to understand you and give you satisfactory answers. If your questions are long and complicated, you're likely to get either a blank stare of incomprehension or an apologetic 'I'm sorry, but I don't understand what you are getting at.' If you persist in asking complex questions, the interviewees will eventually suspect that you are pretending to know more about the subject than you really do or that you are trying to trick them; either way, they are going to become hostile.

Sometimes your interviewee may be awkward and for some reason refuse to answer your questions. As we shall see later, you have to ask yourself why this is so and find ways of overcoming such resistance. Trick questions that put interviewees in the position of answering against their will might seem to be a good idea at the time, and interviewers do use them. Before you do so, remember that the interviewee can later deny the answer or claim to have been tricked into giving it, which will then diminish its effect and put you in a bad light.

No matter how simply and clearly the questions are framed, distortions can still occur when, for example, the interviewee is afraid of disagreeing with the answer suggested by the interviewer or is eager to please the interviewer and therefore gives the answer expected.

INTERVIEWER: This job is not for strict clock-watchers. How do you feel about doing overtime?
INTERVIEWEE: I don't mind [*when, in fact, the interviewee hates the idea!*].

Distortions can also occur when the interviewee is bored and impatient to finish the interview, so make sure your questions are interesting, stimulating and worded in such a way that the interviewee can develop the answers fully, freely and willingly.

Write down the questions that must be answered. Don't trust to memory, especially when conducting your first interviews, because you may find yourself sitting there in embarrassed silence, knowing there are important points still to be covered but unable to think of the right questions to ask. Your interviewees will be equally embarrassed and only when they have gone will you remember what you wanted to ask, but by then it will be too late. Therefore, instead of trying to commit them to memory, which is never very satisfactory, note down the main questions where they can be easily referred to.

In Chapter 2 I mentioned that the interview can be likened to a play: you and the interviewee are the actors, the room where the interview takes place the stage. Actors play the same role on the stage night after night; you may be called on to interview only now and then, so you cannot be expected to remember your script without a prompt. Which is why I recommend that you write down the main questions. You will have a good idea of the shape of the interview and, with this list in a convenient place where you can glance at it without disturbing the interviewee, you will never be caught off guard. Confident that a quick glance at the questions will tell you what to ask next, you will be able to conduct the interview in a relaxed and calm manner, and your lack of nervousness will have a salutary effect on your interviewee, who will feel at ease and respond readily to your questions.

Don'ts

Here is a check-list of the kinds of questions to avoid:

- leading questions
- trick questions
- vague questions
- jargon-loaded questions
- impertinent questions
- sarcastic questions.

Leading questions. This is one of the most problematic kinds of question, because, although you can recognize one when you see one, they can be extremely difficult to avoid asking unless you are on guard against them.

What is a leading question? In our courts, judges come down heavily on counsels who try to force witnesses to answer such questions as 'When did you last beat your wife?' and 'Where were you standing when you hit the complainant?'

In the first example, no matter how he answers, the witness is caught in the trap of having to admit he beat his wife; in the second the witness must admit to hitting the complainant. In neither case is the witness given the freedom to answer, 'I did not beat my wife/hit the complainant.'

As in court, so in interviews: the leading question traps interviewees into giving the answer the interviewer wants, not necessarily the one they may wish to give. When asked, 'Were you popular at school?', the interviewee is hardly likely to endanger the chance of getting a job by answering 'No.' If the interviewer says, 'I see you specialized in mathematics. I expect that's because you found it easier than the others,' the interviewee is being forced by the interviewer to admit that mathematics was the only subject he or she was any good at. The two objectives of questions are to obtain accurate information and to motivate the interviewee to respond freely, and a leading question negates both.

Trick questions. These questions are asked not to obtain information but to trap interviewees into making admissions they may not wish to make, and are therefore similar in results to leading questions.

INTERVIEWER [*to male interviewee*]: How would you react if a woman you thought had fewer qualifications than yourself was suddenly made your boss?

The manner in which this question is phrased is loaded against the interviewee. It may be that he has neither thought of the matter nor, if he had, has any objections to a woman as his boss. By adding the clause 'you thought had fewer qualifications than yourself', you trap him into making admissions that might well go against his real feelings about working for a woman.

It is wise to remember that the interviewee is not your opponent and that, in the majority of interviews, you are ostensibly on the same side, aiming at the same goal. Trick questions, therefore, ought not to have any place in the process. Having said that, I realize that there are situations where it might be necessary to probe deeper into the interviewee's replies, but this should be done by asking searching questions that penetrate the bland clichés the interviewee may be feeding you.

INTERVIEWER [*to job applicant*]: Why did you apply for this job?
INTERVIEWER: I like working with people.
INTERVIEWER: When you say that, what exactly do you mean?

Vague questions. Clichés, as in 'What is it you want out of life?' lead to vagueness. Few people have got themselves, let alone their hopes and ambitions, so clearly worked out that they can answer such a question. If an interviewee does manage to come up with a reply, it will probably be couched in another cliché, for example: 'I want to make the most of myself/develop myself as far as my potential will allow.'

The insincerity of such an answer should be obvious, for it is giving what the interviewee thinks the interviewer wants to hear. The truth is probably a mixture of many things, too complicated to simplify on the spot. 'Ers' and 'Umms' and a few confused and misleading thoughts off the top of the interviewee's head would be a more honest but equally unhelpful response.

The interviewer's question could be better put as 'How do you see yourself in five years' time?' or 'What are your long-term goals?' These queries are more precise and will encourage the interviewee to give a more thoughtful reply.

Jargon-loaded questions. It should never be the object of an interviewer to impress the interviewee. The experienced interviewer will try to adapt his or her language and terminology to the interviewee's background and experience without being patronizing. Good questions, therefore, are phrased in terms the interviewee can understand.

The only time when the use of jargon is acceptable is when it is shared by both participants, for example two people working in the same profession. Thus, one construction engineer interviewing another who is applying for a job may ask questions about past work experience that will be unintelligible to the outsider but make perfectly good sense to the interviewee. Questions expressed in a jargon that only the interviewer understands are asked not to obtain information but to show the interviewee how much the interviewer knows about the subject. In other words, their function is to impress. The interviewer would receive blank stares for answers.

Impertinent questions. It is obvious that you should not ask such questions. The problem is identifying the kind of question that the interviewee may perceive as impertinent, which comes down to: are you able to empathize with the interviewee?

Empathy is the ability to see things from the other person's point of view, and without it an interview can flounder, as was the case when a cocky young reporter asked a famous actress, 'Do you ever think of sex?', to which she icily replied, 'Since you entered the room, I haven't given it a moment's thought.' A question that may seem perfectly right and proper to the interviewer may be considered ill-mannered by the interviewee, for example: 'I only know your neighbourhood by reputation. Pretty rough, is it?'

An interviewee could regard it as an impertinence to be addressed by his or her first name and you should not do so unless, as the interview proceeds, a cordiality develops between you and the interviewee, in which case it is allowable only if you first ask the interviewee's permission.

Sarcastic questions. One person's sarcasm is another's pain. Sarcasm hurts; that's why people use it. Sarcasm makes a point; it does not obtain information.

Sarcasm, whatever the purpose, should always be avoided. Interviewers who find themselves resorting to it usually lack the sensitivity to see how their questions are affecting the interviewee and are then astonished when the interviewee responds aggressively or resentfully towards them. If the intention is to call an employee to order because a company rule has been broken, using sarcasm will cause anger rather than a desire to correct the fault and fall into line. Where, for example, an employee has been persistently late for work, it is important that the manager finds out the real reason so that the fault can be corrected. The employee may be having serious problems with drugs or alcohol. Employees may desperately want to discuss the problem with someone because they recognize their need for help. The manager who, intending to make a friendly joke, starts out with a question like 'Who's the lucky girl, then? Who's been keeping you busy at night?', trivializes the issue, and the employee may be forgiven for feeling that the manager is not going to take the problem seriously.

4.   QUESTION STRATEGY

Having examined what questions to ask and what not to ask, we are going to consider *how* to ask the right questions and the strategy you employ to make sure that you are:

- in control
- keeping your interviewee involved and on course
- getting the information you require to fulfil the purpose of the interview.

Decide on the order of your main questions in advance. Have you ever dried up in a job interview? You cannot think of another question to ask, so you and the interviewee sit staring at each other with blank faces, neither of you knowing what to do next. To end the agony you hurriedly mutter, 'Well, we seem to have covered everything.' Relieved, the interviewee gets up and leaves –

and then you remember you haven't asked when the interviewee will be available to take up the offered post.

Such a situation is embarrassing and inefficient, but easily avoidable. If your script is worked out in advance and you have your main questions in the appropriate order on a sheet of paper placed in a position where you can see them at a glance (for example on a clipboard, which you hold on your lap), you should never be at a loss to know what to ask next. You will have the confidence to handle any awkward situation that may arise. Some authorities suggest learning these questions by rote to give you the appearance of even greater confidence and control. I don't agree with this idea, because it puts an extra burden on you. You are concentrating on what you have learnt at the same time as trying to conduct the interview and listening to what the interviewee is saying. You are more likely to dry up if you are trying to remember what questions come next than if you know you can easily read them off.

Getting the pace of the interview right is a vital part of control and, by working out in advance the best order in which to ask your questions, you can take the interviewee through the various stages at the right tempo.

Start with the easy ones. The sooner you can get your interviewees to talk about themselves the better, because there is nothing like the sound of their own voices to give them confidence. Start, therefore, with uncontroversial questions, which the interviewees ought to be able to handle easily, on those topics that relate to positive aspects of themselves.

For the job interview, this should be quite simple, because you have numerous areas of mutual interest to explore, such as work experience.

INTERVIEWER: I'm very interested in what you said in your application form about your experience with Jones & Co. Could we begin by talking about your duties in your last position as senior planner?

If the interview relates to a problem or involves disciplining the interviewee, you should still strive to find some positive topic to start with. You may later have to dwell on negative aspects, but it is a mistake to go straight for them, because the interviewee will perceive this as a personal attack and respond either by attacking back, which, considering your relative positions of power, is unlikely, or, as is more likely, by becoming withdrawn and closing up.

What you want is to reduce, not increase, the distance between you, which a direct question relating to something the interviewee may be ashamed of or embarrassed by is bound to do.

INTERVIEWER: What project are you working on at the moment?
not
INTERVIEWER: Your work lately has been very poor. How do you account for this?

Phrase questions positively. If you want the interviewee to answer positively and with confidence you too must convey an air of confidence. The way you sit, the way you talk and the way you conduct yourself generally will give this impression. Much also depends on the manner in which you phrase your questions, which should be positively and with conviction, as in 'Could you tell me . . .' and not apologetically, as in 'I wonder if you could perhaps tell me . . .'

Focus on new areas of interest. Before the interview, endeavour to find out as much about the interviewee as possible by consulting the relevant documents, the application form or staff records, and do not waste precious time asking basic questions, the answers to which are in those documents. What interviewees want is the opportunity to express themselves on those topics they regard as most important, not to go over material that is, or should be, known to you.

So, in an employment interview ask questions that focus on new areas of interest and make that focus as sharp as possible. A vague opening question, such as 'I'd like you to tell me a bit about yourself' is bound to get the answer 'What do you want to know?', while 'Tell me about your school career' would probably prompt the response 'Where do you want me to begin?'

These unfocused questions waste time and give the impression that you have not prepared yourself properly for the interview and are desperately floundering around, looking for something to ask. If you have already gone through the application form, which you should have in front of you, you should start by asking questions that have not been sufficiently covered by it.

INTERVIEWER: You say in your application form that in your last job you did not feel you received the recognition you deserved. Why do you think this was the case?

In a disciplinary interview you do not want to dwell on the interviewee's past difficulties, unless, of course, they are related in some way to the present problem. Start by asking about the new, not the old, problems. It signals to the interviewee that you have not made a prejudgement and are determined to deal promptly and effectively with the present complaint.

Move from the general to the specific. As part of the process of putting the interviewee in the picture, as well as keeping the interview stimulating both for yourself and the interviewee, it is a good policy to develop your question strategy in such a way that you outline the general area of your interest and then move step by step through the specific aspects you want to discuss.

A doctor's interview with a patient is a good example of how this strategy works. In the first instance the doctor usually asks, 'What is the problem?', to which the patient replies, 'Well, doctor, I've not been feeling too well lately' or 'I have this pain.' The doctor then, step by step, elicits from the patient precisely, or as near precisely as possible, what the symptoms are and from that information makes a diagnosis.

This is how it could work in a job interview, in which your questions should not be so wide ranging that they cannot be dealt with adequately by the interviewees. Give them the necessary guidance by telling them where you want them to begin.

INTERVIEWER: Let's look at your recent school career, starting with your A levels. What made you choose maths, physics, English and German?

Once this general question has been answered, it will be followed, if necessary, with questions about the particular subjects, such as 'You say you found maths a challenge. What do you mean by that?'

Moving from the general to the specific is the best way to ensure receiving detailed answers that are free of bland clichés and vague generalizations.

Complete one area before going on to the next. Interviewees are trying to tell you a story, be it about a past career, the problems they are facing or the product they are selling or buying. The interviewer's questions should help interviewees to tell that story in the most logical and ordered fashion. Leaping back and forth from one subject to another will only be confusing and distracting, so deal with one subject at a time; only when you feel you have adequately covered it should you pass on to the next.

If, while the interviewee is answering a question on a new subject, you suddenly remember a question you ought to have asked on a previous topic, do not interrupt. Let the interviewee finish properly and then, with a brief explanation, return to the question you ought to have asked. You can, if you prefer, leave the unasked question till the end of the interview, but make a note of it, otherwise you may forget it.

Keep the information flowing. As you will by now have gathered, the best questions are those that allow the interviewee the chance to answer freely and fully. Questions that demand only a 'Yes' or 'No' do not fall into this category, and they should be avoided, unless it is merely to clear up some factual point.

One sure way of avoiding 'closed' questions, as they are sometimes called, is to preface your questions with the journalist's stand-by, the five Ws: Who, Where, When, What and Why, to which you can add How. Most questions prefaced with any of those interrogatories, especially the last three, will yield an 'open' reply. For instance, the question 'Did you know that . . . ?' will elicit the response 'Yes' or 'No'. If it is phrased 'How did you find out . . . ?' it will give the interviewee the opportunity to answer at some length.

If in seeking the interviewee's opinion you ask, 'Are you in favour of . . .' you will again receive a closed response, whereas 'What is your view of . . . ?' will require a much more detailed reply.

Asking the hard ones. Much as you would prefer your interviews to go smoothly, with the interviewee giving full and detailed answers to all your questions, it sometimes happens that the interviewee, for one reason or another, does not wish to answer you in full or at all. What do you do then?

To some interviewers the solution is obvious: put the interviewees under stress by asking the same question repeatedly until they crack. Indeed, in the employment interview, deliberately creating stress has been recommended by some authorities as the best way of testing the interviewee's ability to stand up to the pressures and strains of the job.

Stress produces anxiety, fear and aggression, which are not exactly conducive to maintaining rapport. At best, they put a distance between you and the interviewee; at worst, they can completely ruin the interview.

An interview is not a chance to show how tough, forceful or sharp-witted you are, nor is it an excuse for an argument or a debate. Its purpose is to get information from the interviewee without turning it into a clash of wills. It is not your job to protect the interviewees from the truth or to encourage them to hide behind vague answers. If it is important that you should know more than an interviewee chooses to tell, then you have to probe for the truth and at the same time try not to destroy anyone's dignity and self-respect.

Ask the questions, even if they may embarrass the interviewee, but leave them until you feel you have established sufficient rapport and try as far as possible to spread them throughout the interview rather than clustering them together. You should not start off with controversial questions, because that will merely create distance between you and the interviewee, which you will then have to work at reducing.

If the question is likely to be embarrassing you can give the interviewee some warning, but you should not show embarrassment, either by a change in your tone of voice or by averting your eyes. You should endeavour to ask the tricky ones in the same cool, detached and unemotional way that you would ask any question.

INTERVIEWER: Dealing now with your past experience, I see in your application that between the years 19— and 19— you were out of work, but you don't say why. Could you give more details of what happened during that period?

INTERVIEWER: I notice that you did not complete your degree. What was the reason for this?

Always give the interviewee time to answer and, even if there is a long pause, do not jump in with the next question. As we shall see later, silence after a searching question is entirely appropriate and fulfils the useful purpose of indicating that you are waiting for a full, honest reply. Remember, it is not your job to get the interviewee off the hook. If, however, the silence goes on too long, you may have to probe further to find out whether the interviewee genuinely does not have an answer or is trying desperately to think up one that will satisfy you. If you think the hesitation is caused by embarrassment, you should reassure the interviewee that it is safe to give you the answer because nothing the interviewee says will either shock or astonish you.

A colleague told me of an interview with a brash, handsome young man who had applied to her for a job. The interview had been going well until she reached a point that had been worrying her and the following interchange took place:

INTERVIEWER: As I understand it, you were made redundant when others junior to you in your department kept their jobs. I know this may be difficult for you to talk about, but why do you think this happened?

INTERVIEWEE: The head of my department also left.

INTERVIEWER: I don't see the connection.

INTERVIEWEE: I was living with her.

5. USE OF THE VOICE

The importance of the effective use of the voice cannot be overestimated. Here, again, the similarity between the interview and a stage production comes to mind. Actors know how to deliver their lines so that the audience is kept interested in what they are saying. The same applies to the interviewer and interviewee. The effect of an interviewer's question can be spoilt if asked in the wrong manner. It is not enough that interviewers know what questions to ask; they also have to ask them in such a way that the interviewee understands and responds to them.

Noisy interviewers, consciously or unconsciously, take the spotlight away from the interviewee and concentrate it upon themselves, just like the actor who hams up a part to the detriment of the other performers.

If the interviewer's voice is too loud or too strident, the interviewee may be intimidated by it or resent its intrusiveness. If, on the other hand, the interviewer's voice is too soft and diffident, the interviewee is not going to feel much respect for or be reassured by the interviewer and may be tempted to take control of the interview.

Your tone of voice, therefore, should convey a sense of assurance and confidence without sounding bullying and hectoring. Nor should it remain monotonously the same throughout the interview, but should be modulated to suit the circumstances. For instance, when putting questions of a less serious nature, it can be lighter and higher than for serious questions. This will keep the interviewee interested and alert.

Most important, your voice should always be audible. Speak clearly at a moderate pace and turn towards interviewees so that they can hear you and see your expression. As we shall see below in the discussion of body language, non-verbal communication through facial expressions can be just as important as the spoken word.

It is distracting for interviewees to have to strain to catch a mumbled question directed at their feet, and, because it is very embarrassing to have to keep asking for a question to be repeated, they will only do so once or twice, after which the answers will be based on what they think you asked. Communication between you will have been seriously compromised and the result is confusion.

Just as a physical twitch is distracting, so is a verbal mannerism, such as 'Umm' and 'Ahh', and the constant repetition of phrases like 'You know' or 'Well' or, a more recent addition to that ever growing stockpile of verbal twitches, 'Know what I mean.' Rather than concentrating on the question, the interviewee will start anticipating when you are about to say the phrase again and may even be counting how many times it is repeated!

We can use our voices to ease the interview along and encourage the interviewee without actually saying much. Appropriate reactions of pleasurable surprise, such as 'I see!', 'Really!', 'Very interesting!' and 'I understand', can be very gratifying to an interviewee. There is also that large range of grunts and murmurs like 'Uh-huh' or 'Mm-mm', accompanied by nods, which convey your continuing interest and involvement and help give the interviewees confidence in what they are saying.

6. BODY LANGUAGE

Control through asking questions involves spoken language, and there is another language that is used by the interviewer to direct the interview that is just as necessary and just as effective: body language, or what the psychologists call 'non-verbal communication'.

From the moment an interview begins, the interviewees are looking to you, the interviewer, for clues as to how they are doing, whether it is your approval they want, your advice, your sympathy or merely – in the fact-finding interview – confirmation that you have understood what they have told you. You, in turn, feed them these clues mainly in non-verbal ways: by the way you sit, hold your head, direct your eyes and make noises in your throat.

Much of the time, in normal relationships with others, we are not aware of the signals we give out, which is probably just as well, otherwise we would become self-conscious and start giving the wrong signs. But as we have already seen, the interview is a deliberately contrived relationship, therefore the signals we give as interviewers should be more deliberate. Everything you do and every gesture you make that succeeds in motivating the interviewees is good; everything you do that distracts them is bad.

The importance of the right seating arrangement should now

become clear. The interviewees must be seated where, if they wish, they can see your body movements without undue strain. They are looking to you to see how you are receiving the information they are giving you, so your posture, like your voice, should reflect openness and a willingness to listen. Sitting rigidly or hunched up with your arms folded conveys unease and rejection; an interviewee will probably soon do the same, as experiments have shown that the interviewee imitates the posture of the interviewer. This will create a distance between you that words alone will not bridge.

Fidgeting, slouching, rocking, biting your lips, turning away, tapping fingers or pencils – all these, whether you realize it or not, signal lack of interest, inattentiveness or impatience. All are distracting; all should be avoided.

Facial expressions too speak louder than words. By looking interested you are encouraging the interviewee to answer your questions fully. By reacting appropriately, for example smiling at the right time or looking concerned, you are showing the interviewee that you are attending to what is being said. When the interviewee makes a particularly interesting point or you are waiting for an answer to be completed, lean forward. The occasional nod of the head or holding your chin in your hand will also convey that you are giving your undivided attention.

Some gestures, however, should be avoided. In a problem-solving interview, for instance, if the interviewee in seeking advice from you has to tell you something about his or her private life, which may not necessarily meet with your approval, reacting with a frown reveals your displeasure. Natural though this may be, it is inappropriate for an interview in which you are required to make an objective assessment of the situation. Similarly, shaking your head, clicking your tongue or any other gesture that indicates disapproval or censure is to be avoided, because as an interviewer it is not your job to act as counsel for the prosecution.

7. EYE CONTACT

The interviewees, while answering your questions, need to know whether or not you are attending to what they are saying, whether you have understood it, agreed with it or disagreed and whether to carry on or not. In other words, they want to know how you are reacting to them but cannot actually ask you, so instead they look at you, concentrating most of the time on your eyes.

Eye contact is thus an essential part of non-verbal communication. If you look back at interviewees in an interested way, they will be motivated to respond positively to your questions. On the other hand, if your eyes are fixed on some distant point in the room or are gazing down at your hands or the desk, they will consider that you are not interested in their answers and will become taciturn and uncooperative.

Eye contact should not be overdone. A look, if carried on too long, can become a stare or a gaze. A stare is threatening and a gaze is embarrassing because it may suggest an inappropriate interest in the interviewee. Both will be distracting. Look expectantly at interviewees when you ask your questions, but also glance away so as not to inhibit them, which you might do if you fix your gaze on them all the time, especially if they are having trouble answering a question. Look back again for another brief period and away, and so on, till they have finished answering. If your look is accompanied by the occasional nod of the head, the approving 'Hm-mm, I see, I understand', you will be giving interviewees all the feedback they need to reassure them that you approve of what they are saying.

8. THE ART OF GOOD LISTENING

'You have two ears and only one mouth, so you should listen twice as much as you should talk,' as an old teacher of mine once said. To which I would add: 'Without good listening there is no direction and without direction there is no effective interviewing.'

Listening to answers is just as important as asking questions, and, like asking questions and body language, it is one of the least obvious and obtrusive techniques whereby the interviewer controls the interview.

One way to judge whether an interview has been effective is to compare the amount of talking done by the interviewer with that of the interviewee. If the interviewer hogs the time with long questions and a lot of chit-chat in between, leaving little room for the interviewee, the interview will probably be a failure. As I have mentioned before, good interviewers should spend no more than fifteen per cent of the time talking; the rest belongs exclusively to the interviewee.

There is listening and good listening. Sitting in stony silence or not concentrating on what is being said is probably as bad as not listening at all, because the effect is the same. It takes a dedicated egotist to be able to talk in the face of indifference or boredom and the interviewees will quickly dry up if they think you are not interested.

If they can see from the expression on your face and from your gestures that you are paying attention to everything they say, they will experience this as a figurative pat on the back or a reward, and will be encouraged to continue giving you full answers. If they see boredom, lack of interest or disapproval in your expressions or gestures, they will withdraw into themselves, hide their feelings and give you only brief, unhelpful replies.

Good listening is more than just registering the words uttered by the interviewee. You are not merely a tape recorder. To listen properly and to hear not only what the interviewees are telling you but also what they are not takes concentration and intelligence, as well as humility and patience. It is the ability to hear the feelings expressed by the interviewee behind the words, as well as any omissions and evasions.

INTERVIEWER: Why did you leave your last employment?
INTERVIEWEE: I wasn't too happy there.
   [*Here the good listener will immediately be alerted to an evasion and probe for more information.*]
INTERVIEWER: Why weren't you happy?
INTERVIEWEE: I didn't get along with some of the staff.
INTERVIEWER: Why not? What was the problem?
INTERVIEWEE: Well, you see, I don't consider myself a world-beater.
   [*Behind the cliché, the interviewee is expressing an attitude about himself in relation to others that needs further explanation.*]

INTERVIEWER: What do you mean by that?

INTERVIEWEE: Well, frankly, when the pace is too hard, I can't keep up. And they make fun of me.

Good listening does not come naturally, but like good interviewing it improves with practice. It is something you can – and should – practise every time you are in conversation with another person.

Before analysing what makes a good listener, let us see what errors bad listeners make.

1. They hear what they want to hear, not what the interviewee is saying.

2. They listen only to those details that interest them and switch off for the rest.

3. They are unable to put themselves into the interviewee's shoes and cannot really understand what feelings the interviewee is expressing.

4. They may be too sympathetic to the interviewee's point of view, so that they cannot listen objectively to what the interviewee is saying.

5. They are too involved with their own thoughts and problems to concentrate on those of the interviewee.

6. They have not prepared themselves well enough in advance and while they should be listening they are thinking up the next question.

7. They are easily distracted by the interviewee's mannerisms, dress, accent and so on.

8. They lack patience and will not let the interviewee finish answering properly.

Now, what about good listeners?

1. They have sufficient empathy to create the best surroundings, which permit the interviewees to give their best.

2. They have prepared themselves so that they have the freedom and confidence to devote time and energy to listening to what is being said by the interviewee rather than worrying about whether they are asking the right questions to get the information they require.

3. They have worked out in advance the main questions they intend to ask and in what order so that they can impose upon the interview a shape to which the interviewee can respond and feel at ease with.

4. They have cultivated the ability to listen behind the words and to catch the nuances of meaning, the words emphasized, the hesitations, uncertainties, omissions and inconsistencies that tell them more than just the words.

5. They have the persistence and patience to probe the interviewee with further questions until the interviewee understands that the omissions and evasions have been noted and that further information must be forthcoming to satisfy the interviewer.

6. They have the maturity and insight to remain objective and not to impose their own views on what the interviewee is saying, while they recognize that what the interviewee is relating are events and experiences subjectively interpreted by the interviewee.

7. They talk as little as possible, concentrate as much as possible and show the interviewee by expressions and gestures that they are taking everything in.

INTERVIEWEE: I don't think I will ever get promoted.
INTERVIEWER: Why do you say that?
INTERVIEWEE: I reckon I'm too old.

(At this point the good listeners should be asking themselves, 'Is that really what the interviewee is thinking or is age being used as a cover-up for some other inadequacy?' If the reason is the former, they should feel able to reassure the interviewee; if the latter, they need to probe further.)

8. They have the patience to allow the interviewee to complete the answers, even when the interviewee is struggling to articulate them. This is particularly important if the interviewee's cultural or educational background differs substantially from the interviewer's.

9. In interviews with additional stress, such as a problem-solving interview, they are able to tolerate emotional outbursts, weeping, anger and hostility, even directed against themselves, and can accept that it is probably not personal but aimed at those they represent or at the world at large. They do not leave it at that, however. By listening and probing further they may reveal the source of the hostility and help the interviewee to find ways of resolving it.

10. They accept that, although they might not like what the interviewee is saying nor the interviewee, they must be tolerant enough to put personal feelings aside. They continue to give the interviewee the same amount of encouragement and attention as they would if the interviewee were a close friend.

    Where time is limited, good listeners must be more than usually well prepared so that they do not have to waste precious moments covering matters that are either irrelevant to the purpose of the interview, or can be found out elsewhere.

(A word of caution: it is doing a disservice both to you and to your interviewees to plan a day of interviewing that allows you no time to be quietly on your own between interviews. If you do not give yourself a chance to recover from one interview before going on to the next, with the best will in the world you will start to find your concentration flagging and good listening will become increasingly difficult. When you have to interview a number of people on one day, take as many short breaks between interviews as possible to refresh yourself so that you can face the next interviewee with renewed energy and interest.)

Taking Notes

To take notes or not to take notes? This vexed question has been debated in the literature of interviewing over the years. It is generally acknowledged that notes do fulfil a useful function, if only as an aid to memory. Most of us have limited memories, especially when it comes to recalling what people have told us; if we have no record of an interview and have to rely entirely on our memories, we are bound to make mistakes.

In job interviewing, to base the choice of an applicant on memory alone when faced with half a dozen applicants in as many hours is asking the impossible. By the end of the last interview you will have forgotten almost everything of importance that was said in the first interview and you will remember only those details that, if you liked the applicants, were in their favour, and, if you disliked them, were to their disadvantage. This phenomenon is known as the 'halo effect'.

Interviewers who claim that they never need to take a note because they remember everything are generally the ones who are quickest at making a decision about the interviewee – sometimes before the interviewee has had a chance of saying anything – and they are frequently wrong in their assessments.

The problem is that we are very good at forgetting details, or rather that we remember what we want to remember and forget details that seem irrelevant or unimportant because they do not accord with our own experience. If a job applicant shares with the interviewer an interest in, say, rugby, the interviewer may tend to forget when making an assessment that the applicant's previous experience was not nearly as relevant as the experience of another applicant who collected stamps.

We also tend to remember details that confirm our own beliefs and forget those that go against them. After an appraisal interview, a manager may forget that the employee had some very good suggestions about improving efficiency in the department and remember only the employee's slovenly clothes and arrogant and pushy demeanour.

Finally, we often forget things that conflict with our own interests. Even when we tell people about our lives, we prefer to leave out details from our past that we perceive to be awkward or embarrassing and conflict with how we now wish to present ourselves to the world. It is not exactly lying; we just alter the facts by tidying up loose ends to make a more positive, attractive and (we like to think) coherent picture from the confused muddle that is reality.

In all kinds of interviewing it is safer to take notes and not to rely on an imperfect memory, especially if you are interviewing a number of people in a day.

The use of a tape recorder has been recommended by some as an alternative to note-taking, but there is still a resistance to them, both by management and staff, and for a good reason. When reporters go out on an interview with a tape recorder, they will probably never see the interviewee again. Management and staff, however, are in day-to-day contact and the notion of employees' words being committed permanently to tape and, it may be feared, used against them is not conducive to a trusting relationship.

The only problem about taking notes is how to do so without distracting the interviewee. What distracts is the actual process of writing and the break in eye contact while it is taking place. It results in an unnatural hiatus, during which the interviewee is suspended in limbo, waiting for the next question. It behoves the interviewer, therefore, to make the break as natural and as least disruptive as possible. Here are some hints on how to take notes.

1. Never try to hide the fact that you are taking notes. Rather, draw the interviewee's attention to what you are doing by first asking permission, blaming the need to do so on your own faulty memory.

    INTERVIEWER [*at the start of the interview*]: Do you mind if, while we're talking, I jot down a few points? It's just so I won't forget anything important you tell me.
    INTERVIEWER [*during the interview*]: That's very interesting. I'd like to make a note of it, if you don't mind.

2. Keep the pad where it is easy to reach, such as attached to a clipboard on a desk or table or on your knees. Always make

sure you have a pen handy – and that it works! An interviewer shuffling papers on the desk, looking for a pen and finding one that does not write is acting very unprofessionally and such antics will be very distracting to the interviewee.

3. Limit your note-taking to the most important material and do not bother with information that is already on record. Keep notes brief to minimize loss of eye contact.

4. Take notes about facts and not about intimate personal details, otherwise interviewees may be justified in thinking that you are keeping the information to use against them at a later stage. For example, if the interviewee tells you that he is in the process of divorcing his wife, that is not the time to jot down 'is divorcing his wife'.

5. Always put the interviewee's words in quotation marks to distinguish them from your own comments, because, when you come to refer to them later, it may be important to remember who made which remark.

6. If you intend to write up the interview based on your notes, do so as soon as is practicable after the interview. The notes are bound to be brief (unless you are very adept at shorthand), and you may need to add details from memory (faulty though it may be) in order to obtain a reasonably full and fair picture of what was said and what your impressions were.

7. Some authorities suggest that in job interviewing the task of assessing the candidate's suitability will be eased if the interviewer fills in a standard graded form during the course of the interview. The grades relate to the areas covered by the application form, such as the interviewee's educational background, qualifications and job experience, and to individual characteristics, social relationships and the impact the interviewee made on the interviewer. Alternatively, notes taken during the interview can be expanded on to a standard form directly after the interview.

9. SPECIAL TECHNIQUES

What do you do if:

- you are not getting the answers you want
- they are not as complete as you'd like them to be
- you think the interviewee may be deliberately omitting information to mislead you
- you think he or she may be lying?

These are some common problems that occur in interviews, which the following special probing techniques will help you overcome.

Focusing

Start with a general question and gradually narrow the focus until the interviewee is forced to concentrate more specifically on a particular aspect of the topic that you are interested in. It is more difficult for the interviewee to evade your questions, as in this example from a problem-solving interview.

INTERVIEWER: How are you getting on?
INTERVIEWEE: OK.
INTERVIEWER: No problems?
INTERVIEWEE: Well, I've been getting lots of headaches lately.
INTERVIEWER: Headaches? What do you think caused them?
INTERVIEWEE: I've had a bit of trouble with the new computer.
INTERVIEWER: What trouble is that?

(And so it goes on until it emerges that the interviewee's struggle to learn how to operate the computer was causing stress, which in turn caused the headaches. The problem having been revealed, the interviewer is now in a position to help solve it.)

Or in this job interview:

INTERVIEWER: What were your reasons for leaving your last job?
INTERVIEWEE: I didn't think I was being appreciated.
INTERVIEWER: In what way weren't you appreciated?
INTERVIEWEE: They didn't pay me what I deserved.

Summarizing

When you think the interviewees are deliberately omitting some important information or where you feel they could give you more details, going over their previous answer(s) helps you to see the gaps more clearly and encourages them to fill them in.

INTERVIEWER: Now, let's see if I've got this right: you said that you have never been unemployed, but then you also said that after you left college you did not work for six months. Is that correct?

INTERVIEWEE: Oh, yes, I didn't think it was important.

INTERVIEWER: What did you do during that period?

INTERVIEWEE: Oh, I travelled around Europe.

INTERVIEWER: That must have been interesting. What sort of experience do you think you gained from it?

Whatever reply the interviewee gives, there remains the question why he or she did not think it important enough to mention. Was the interviewee embarrassed, worried about how the interviewer would take it or forgetful? The answer to *that* could give the interviewer valuable insight into the interviewee's personality.

I was told of an interview with a school-leaver who was applying for a place in a college. He was a considerable French scholar and was reading Proust in the original in the train on his way to the interview, but to the question. 'What sort of reading do you like?' he replied that he did not read very much. As reading was an occupation much valued by the college, he did not receive an offer of a place. Later, when asked why he did not mention the French novel, he said he thought it would sound pretentious and that the interviewer would penalize rather than praise him.

I think the interviewer was at fault for not hearing the unspoken doubt in the interviewee's reply and probing further, thus:

INTERVIEWER: You don't read at all?

INTERVIEWEE: Well, a bit – in French.

INTERVIEWER: What sort of books, novels, non-fiction?

INTERVIEWEE: Novels, mainly.

INTERVIEWER [*impressed but not convinced*]: Could you perhaps give me some titles?

In probing exercises, always remember Kipling's six honest serving-men who taught him all he knew – 'Their names are What and Why and When and How and Where and Who' – and you will never be at loss for a follow-up question.

Summarizing also helps to put the interviewees back in the picture if they have gone astray during the previous answer, and, of course, helps you if you have lost your way. If the interview is long and arduous and it covers many topics, occasional summaries keep it moving along at a good pace; if, despite your precautions, there is an interruption, such as a telephone ringing, you should make a summary of the last points before continuing.

Rephrasing or Restating

Rephrasing is a useful device, which reminds the interviewees that they have not given you all you need and at the same time encourages them to be more forthcoming. All you have to do is repeat some of what they have said in the last reply or state it again in your own words as you have understood it.

INTERVIEWEE: I don't think I'm making much headway in this department.
INTERVIEWER: Not much headway?
INTERVIEWEE: No. I think my supervisor has it in for me.
INTERVIEWER: You don't think he likes you?

Obviously you cannot go on repeating and rephrasing like this, nor will you need to, because interviewees will soon understand that you are not satisfied with their answers and that you require fuller replies to your questions.

With the right kind of emphasis, restating or rephrasing responses can be a subtle but clear indication to the interviewees that you think they are lying. In the example below, the interviewee has not given the reason for leaving the last job. The interviewer, however, suspects the interviewee may have been sacked.

INTERVIEWER: You've not mentioned why you left your last job?
INTERVIEWEE: I didn't get on with my boss.

INTERVIEWER: You quarrelled?

INTERVIEWEE: Well, not exactly. Let's just say we had a disagreement.

INTERVIEWER: A disagreement?

Continuing calmly but persistently in this unemotive manner, the interviewer should ultimately get to the truth, which has to be done before employing the applicant can be considered.

Silence

It is a common mistake to assume that either the interviewer or the interviewee must always be talking and that even the briefest silence will bring the interview to an abrupt halt. Silence can, in fact, be a very useful probing device, but, just as there is good listening and bad listening, so there is the right kind of silence and the wrong.

The wrong kind is an embarrassed one in which the interviewer looks everywhere but at the interviewee. This loss of eye contact causes a breakdown of rapport, which in turn produces an anxious interviewee.

The right kind is an expectant silence: the interviewer looks at the interviewee and perhaps leans forward slightly with an interested expression on his or her face, which encourages the interviewee to fill in the necessary gaps or to correct some misleading information.

A brief pause may be enough for the interviewee to realize that the question has not yet been fully answered, but reassuring eye contact is essential. If you look away or fix your eyes on some distant point in the room, the interviewee will think that you have lost interest and have ceased to care about what he or she has to say.

Putting on the Pressure

We are here in treacherous waters. As we have seen, there has been a great deal of debate about whether building stress into interviews is a good idea. Some experts maintain that for employment interviewing it is a way of testing how the interviewee will react to the pressures of the job; others claim that at best it is irrelevant, because the stresses of interviewing are different from those of the work, and at worst the tension created by it may cause the interviewee to become withdrawn or angry and resentful. Either way, the interviewees will not give a whole and truthful picture of themselves and what they are really like.

Stress may have a place in interviews for jobs in which stress is an essential part of the work, such as in the police force or air traffic control, but then it should only be handled by interviewers trained and experienced in such techniques. In other types of interview, I think deliberately creating stress is counter-productive and should be avoided. A better way of finding out how a job applicant will behave under stress is to look at the application form, which should give you details about past experiences. Taking these as a basis for careful questioning, you should be able to find out what you want to know about how the interviewee *actually* behaved in stressful situations.

INTERVIEWER: This course you were on lasted only one year and yet you had to cover a great deal of work. Could you tell me how you coped?

INTERVIEWEE: Not too badly.

INTERVIEWER: Well, your results bear that out, but how did you find the pressures?

INTERVIEWEE: Gruelling at times.

INTERVIEWER: Could you be more specific?

There are times when it may be necessary to put some pressure on the interviewee to give an answer or a fuller answer to a question, but you still have to do so cautiously, remembering all the while that the purpose is to get an answer, not to show how powerful you are. Power playing should have no part in good interviewing.

Silence can place harmless but effective pressure on the interviewee to respond. Over-used, however, it can be very daunting. I have heard of stress interviews in which the interviewee enters an almost bare room. The interviewee's chair faces a table behind which is seated the interviewer(s). No one utters a word of welcome or an invitation to sit down. The embarrassed interviewee takes a seat and waits. Still nothing happens. The idea presumably is that either the interviewee will maintain equipoise until the interviewer speaks, showing a capacity to withstand stress, or will crack up, showing the opposite. It is doubtful that such interviews still take place, because tests have shown that they are not very effective in determining or predicting future behaviour.

Begin to ask an important question, pause and remain silent, and that silence should weigh heavily enough on the interviewees to make them want to help you by finishing the sentence.

INTERVIEWER: You decided to give up your career in advertising because . . . ?

    [*Silence follows.*]

INTERVIEWEE: Because I could not stand the rat race any longer.

In the following disciplinary interview, the employee has been coming in late every day for the last week and the interviewer has asked for a reason. The interviewee has remained silent.

INTERVIEWER [*after a pause*]: Just take it slowly.

INTERVIEWEE: It's personal. I'd rather not talk about it.

    [*The interviewer continues to remain silent.*]

INTERVIEWEE: Well, I've been having a bit of trouble with my youngest.

INTERVIEWER: What sort of trouble?

INTERVIEWEE: He's been caught playing truant.

INTERVIEWER: I see, and . . .

INTERVIEWEE: Well, I've gone with him each morning to make sure he gets to school.

Interviewing is a stressful enough process for it not to be necessary to build in more. In using these probing techniques, what you have to do is make clear to the interviewees that you are not trying to trick them into giving answers, nor are you trying to force answers from them, but that it is in their interests, as well as yours, to respond fully. The pressure you put on them lies in the questions you ask, how you phrase them and the calm, persistent tone of voice you use.

When you have a reluctant interviewee, persistence is the key to success. That does not mean repeating the same question over and over again: that is interrogation, not interviewing. It means using all the legitimate techniques at your disposal and at the same time reassuring the interviewees that you are not probing for the sake of probing or to show how powerful you are, but that you are genuinely interested in what they have to say.

In the following interview, the interviewee has come to the interviewer to ask for a transfer to another department. As up until recently the interviewee has been getting on well, the interviewer is naturally alerted to problems that may have arisen.

INTERVIEWER: You seemed happy there before. Has anything happened to make you change your mind?

INTERVIEWEE: Nothing. I'd just like a change of scene. I'm finding it a bit boring, to be honest.

INTERVIEWER: Boring? In what way?

INTERVIEWEE: Well, it's these word processors.

INTERVIEWER: You don't like them?

INTERVIEWEE: Well, I might, but I don't feel confident with them.

INTERVIEWER: What about the training programme you went on?

INTERVIEWEE: That's just it! It wasn't long enough.

INTERVIEWER: Then you'd really like some more training?

INTERVIEWEE: Yes.

Humour

Perhaps the most effective lubricant to make interviews more interesting, enjoyable and rewarding is humour – but only if used correctly and appropriately. A remark or joke shared between interviewer and interviewee can break the ice, help maintain rapport, lighten difficult moments, distract the interviewee from embarrassment or awkwardness and deflect hostility. Used incorrectly, it can be very dangerous and destructive.

Humour depends so much on the circumstances that it is impossible to say when it is appropriate to make a joke or what kind of joke to make. It is easier to point out when and in what circumstances humour is wrong. Here are some of the dangers to be aware of.

At the start of the interview, the interviewer may throw off an ill-considered remark in trying to put the interviewee at ease, which the interviewee regards as insulting, demeaning or a sign that the interviewer is not taking the interview seriously.

INTERVIEWER [*to job applicant*]: You've come all the way from [*name a town or suburb*]. Good heavens, that's the other end of the world! You must be keen!

INTERVIEWER [*to employee*]: Now, what this about you wanting to leave us? Don't like the canteen food, eh? Can't say I blame you.

In the first example, the interviewee may be forgiven for thinking that the interviewer is treating the job interview, which is vital to the interviewee, as a joke. In the second, the remark may convince the disgruntled employee that he has good reason for leaving.

Humour should never be forced. Remembering jokes to tell the interviewee when things seem to be slowing down or to overcome an embarrassing moment will usually fail. To be effective, humour should emerge naturally and spontaneously from the subject-matter. Above all, the joke should be a shared one, which will make it seem part of a conversation.

Jokes should never be made against the interviewee. 'Don't even think about it!', as a parking sign warns New York motorists. What may seem funny to you about the interviewee's appearance, accent, history or problem will never seem funny to him or her. If, however the interviewee draws attention to it in a humorous way, you should join in the fun only with the very greatest caution.

The same stricture applies to jokes about the interviewee's family, friends, associates, clubs, interests and, indeed, anything and everything relating to his or her personal life. Even if the joke is meant in the kindliest possible way, even if the interviewee laughs at it, he or she may also secretly resent it and feel that you are not taking the interview seriously.

Jokes should never be made about age, sex, race, colour or

religion, the interviewee's or anyone else's. To this rule there are no exceptions.

Under the Sex Discrimination Act (1975) there are legal prohibitions about what can be said in an interview. Whereas interviewers may know they should not, for example, ask a female job applicant whether she has plans to get married or who will look after her children when she is at work, they may think it innocuous to make a reference to her appearance:

INTERVIEWER: Those bracelets you're wearing. I could hear you all the way down the passage. You'll be able to give people warning that you're on the way.

Similarly, a supposedly humorous remark intended to put an Asian or West Indian applicant at ease can be derogatory and wounding, for example, 'You must love this very hot weather' or 'That's a long name. Quite a tongue-twister!'

Humour, then, is a valuable, if unpredictable, element in the interview. Used in the right place and at the right time it can work wonders in helping you to overcome awkwardness, embarrassment and even hostility. Use it improperly and you may even find yourself in court!

10.   PROBLEMS ARISING IN THE INTERVIEW

In addition to the general problems mentioned above, the following are some specific ones that may occur in the interview. We can, for convenience, divide them into problems caused by the interviewee and by the interviewer.

Firstly, the interviewee:

- tries to take control
- becomes hostile and aggressive
- becomes emotionally upset
- gives inadequate answers or dries up
- can't stop talking.

Secondly, the interviewer:

- does too much talking
- goes off course.

On the face of it, it appears that the interviewees are more often the ones at fault, but this would be a serious misreading of the situation. Usually the interviewees are *reacting* to something the interviewer has done or said, which causes them to become hostile or upset or gives them the chance to take control of the interview. In looking at how to resolve these difficulties if they arise, therefore, we have to consider where the interviewer may have gone wrong and how the faults can be corrected.

The interviewee takes control. We have discussed in some detail above the need for the interviewer to maintain control throughout the interview. If, however, the interviewer lacks confidence, feels intimidated by the interviewee or is ill-prepared for the interview either by not defining its purpose or not drafting out the main questions, the interviewees may take over and direct it where they want it to go.

One sure sign of this happening is when the interviewees are allowed to talk non-stop, whether or not they are saying anything new and interesting. Another is when, in the middle of the interview, the interviewee starts to ask questions, not by way of clarifying the interviewer's questions but as a means, conscious or not, of taking over. The interviewer then becomes the interviewed. A third sign is when the interviewee persistently and deliberately fails to give adequate answers to the questions. (I recall an occasion when a journalist attempted to interview the singer Bob Dylan. It was clear that with his one-word replies – grunts, rather – Dylan was laughing at the interviewer and was in this sense running the interview from the outset.)

It is essential that the interviewee feels relaxed enough to want to ask questions or to answer at greater length than the interviewer anticipated; but there is a great deal of difference between that and taking control, and the difference is you, the interviewer.

An interviewee can, within the first few minutes, pick up from your verbal and non-verbal signals whether or not you are in control of the interview. Even someone unused to being interviewed can sense from the way you hold yourself, from the manner in which you introduce your questions and from the tone of your voice and the expression on your face, whether you have prepared yourself for the interview. The interviewees take their cue from you. If you have an overwhelming need to impress them with your views, you will have to do much of the talking and it will be easy for them to let you get on with it. They will then assume your role as interviewer. If, on the other hand, you have the necessary confidence – the inner strength that comes essentially from being in control of yourself, both mentally and physically – they will sense how far they can go to challenge you should they so wish, without you ever having overtly to put them down. You will appear friendly, helpful and encouraging and will make every effort to establish a rapport, and they will know that you are taking the interview as seriously as they are. Therefore, they will not want to jeopardize the results but rather work with you to achieve them.

If, however, despite this, they still attempt to take over from you, there are methods by which you can reassert control.

Be calm. Do not get angry with the interviewees, because that will only exacerbate your loss of control, or try to bully them into submission, for that will create greater conflict between you. You are not, after all, in a wrestling match, and it is just as well that you remind yourself of this fact if you feel yourself losing your temper.

Be detached. Try to stand back and ask yourself at what point the interviewee led you away from your planned course. Then go back to the last question before that, even if it means stopping the interviewee or yourself in mid sentence, and say, for example, 'We seem to have strayed off the point, so I'd like to go back to . . .'

Be objective. Ask yourself if you have been talking too much and, if so, why. Have you been trying to impress the interviewee, to show how clever you are? Have you allowed the interview to collapse into conversation or debate? If, objectively, the answer to these is 'Yes', stop talking and go back to your prepared questions, from which you must not stray till the interview is over.

The interviewee becomes hostile and aggressive. In certain kinds of interviewing, such as disciplinary, grievance, resigning and dismissal interviewing, you have to assume that the interviewees are going to be under the influence of strong emotions. You are challenging their whole sense of self-worth, possibly their very identity. They will want to defend themselves, to fight back, and, although you may be speaking not on your own behalf but on behalf of others – the company, the people with whom the interviewees work who have found them inadequate for the job – they will still see you as the enemy. For this reason, many managers understandably find such interviewing very stressful and balk at it.

Some would question the need for an interview when the employee is leaving the company, but I believe that managers can sometimes learn more from a disaffected employee about the company and how well, or otherwise, it is run than they can from a contented one. The employee who is resigning to move up the career ladder has probably done the job successfully and may be able to pass on valuable lessons about the job, the department or, indeed, the organization itself. Finding out why an employee acted in a way that led to dismissal may also yield salutary insights into areas of staff relations that otherwise would never come to the surface.

I suggest the risk of hostility and aggression is worth taking, because, with some forethought and planning, strong emotions that may arise can be channelled away from negative personality clashes into more positive areas of discussion. Where a working relationship is about to be ended, you should wish to leave interviewees with a sense of their own dignity. They may not have been right for the job, but this does not mean they are totally worthless.

How, then, do you cope with the hostile interviewee? Once again, as in all difficult interviews, be calm, be objective, be detached.

As far as time permits, try to plan in advance the questions you want to ask so that, no matter how much they try to provoke you into an argument, you have those questions to fall back on.

Aim to establish a good relationship from the start by showing that, whatever has happened, whatever the circumstances that preceded the interview, you are open-minded and, above all, that you are not sitting as judge and jury. It may be that after the interview you will be required to weigh up the facts and make a decision unfavourable to the interviewee – at worst, they may have done something that requires dismissal – but during the interview your concern is to get to the truth of the matter.

As far as possible, limit your questions to the facts. Facts also include how the interviewees felt about an event when it occurred. They will be viewing their feelings in retrospect rather than experiencing them for the first time, so their emotions should not be as sharp and as difficult to control, especially if the interviewees know that you are not attacking them but searching with them for the truth.

INTERVIEWER: As I think you realize, things can't go on like this any longer. The company wants you to have the chance of improving your performance, so I'd like to know what reasons you have for your recent poor output. Reasons, mind, not excuses!

INTERVIEWEE: There is just too much pressure on me. I never have a chance to finish one job before I have to go on to another.

INTERVIEWER: What kind of pressure are you talking about?

If one version of the facts other than the interviewees' is already known to you, then you should put that version to them to elicit their reaction. By doing this, you will give them the opportunity both to explain their points of view and perhaps also to come to understand the events more clearly.

INTERVIEWER: Your supervisor says that you were insolent when she asked you to carry out her order.

INTERVIEWEE: No, I wasn't. All I said was, it wasn't my job. And I still don't think it was.

INTERVIEWER: I follow that, but looking at it from her point of view, how do you think she interpreted it?

INTERVIEWEE: Hmm, well, I suppose she thought I was being cheeky.

INTERVIEWER: OK, let's take this a step further. Why didn't you think it was your job?

It may be that in the course of the interview the interviewee's mood changes suddenly and unexpectedly from amiable to angry. In this case you will have to analyse what you may have said, what question(s) you put that could have caused this change, retrace your steps to that point and start afresh with a better question.

This does not mean that you can never risk putting questions to the interviewee that may embarrass, distress or even provoke anger. Circumstances may demand that you have to, but, if you have established trust between you, this should not have disastrous effects on the outcome of the interview. Much has to do with how you ask the question, at what point you choose to ask it and how you work up to it.

INTERVIEWER: I hope you understand when I ask the next question that it's because I need to have the information, not because I want to pry into your private life. In your application form I notice that there is a gap of a year between your present job and the one before. What is the reason for this?

INTERVIEWEE: I was out of work.

INTERVIEWER: I take it you tried to get employment?

INTERVIEWEE: Yes, but there was nothing around.

INTERVIEWER: That's strange, because we were actively seeking staff in your area. Why did you not apply then?

INTERVIEWEE: Well, the fact is, I was inside.

INTERVIEWER: Inside?

INTERVIEWEE: In prison.

The interviewee becomes emotionally upset. In counselling and problem-solving interviews, the interviewees may have chosen to come to you or you may have requested that they do so because personal problems are preventing them from carrying out their jobs properly and you feel they need to talk to someone. The desired result of such interviews is that, by articulating the problems, the interviewees find their own solutions. However, in the course of doing so, they may display strong emotions, resulting in anger, secretiveness, truculence or even in tears.

The need to remain calm and detached is vital. You must not:

- play at being a psychiatrist
- show excessive sympathy and concern
- react to what you are told in a critical, judgemental manner.

It is never your role to psychoanalyse your interviewee, and you must resist the temptation to do so, since it could be highly dangerous and counter-productive. The questions you put must be aimed at trying to find solutions; they must not pry in the hope of uncovering deeply buried traumas. If the problems are beyond your scope, you must recognize the fact and recommend someone better qualified to help. This, however, should not be someone from whom either you or members of your family have sought assistance, i.e. not your own family doctor or lawyer.

In many cases, your listening alone may be all the interviewees need, because, just by having the chance to talk to an interested individual who knows the right questions to ask about their problems, the interviewees are helped to find their own solutions, which are the only ones that really matter. Solutions imposed rarely work.

Sympathy is something a parent gives a child who falls down and is hurt. Adults in difficulty, perhaps in mental anguish, who come to you for help are not asking for your sympathy, and, even if they are, it is not part of your task to give it to them. Sympathy involves you in the problem, whereas you need to remain detached from it. Your task is to help the interviewee find a solution, and the interview is the main, possibly the only, means by which you can do this. By asking the appropriate questions you will be giving the interviewees the chance to talk about the problem, which in turn will help them to distance themselves from it and see it in a new perspective.

Keeping your distance does not mean that during the interview you remain cold and unfeeling. If the interviewee loses control and bursts into tears, the last thing he wants to hear from you is 'Pull yourself together, old chap!' The interviewee will, in any event, probably feel very embarrassed and awkward for breaking down in front of you. What you have to convey through words, facial expression and gestures is the reassurance that you understand how the interviewee feels; and at the same time it is vital that you keep the interview going, particularly if you yourself have been upset and distracted by this breakdown.

Once you have allowed the interviewee time to recover composure, you should return to where you left off, continuing your questions in an uncritical, but not unfeeling, manner. That is the best reassurance the interviewees can have that you do not condemn or despise them for the outburst. If, by the expression on your face or something you say, they sense that you do, they will withdraw into themselves, become surly and unresponsive, and the thrust and purpose of the interview will have been lost.

The interviewee gives inadequate answers or dries up. There are a number of reasons why this may occur. It may be that your interviewee is shy, inarticulate or just plain awkward; or it may be that your attitude or your questions are at fault; or even a combination of the two. Whatever the reason, it is your responsibility to find out what is wrong and why. You have to stand back and analyse the problem as objectively as possible, which may not be easy, especially if the interview has been going on for some time. Therefore, the sooner you make your analysis the better, because it is up to you (once again!) to solve the problem and save the interview.

If you decide fairly and objectively that the problem is the interviewee, then you have to concentrate your efforts on establishing and maintaining a rapport. Don't take your cue from the interviewee and become surly and unresponsive; rather let the interviewee take the cue from you.

Your attitude should be friendly, businesslike and non-judgemental. The message you convey verbally and non-verbally should be that you are not out to dominate or destroy, to undermine or condemn and that you see the interview as a co-operative enterprise from which you will both gain. Even very shy individuals are likely to respond positively to someone who appears to be interested in who they are and what they have to say. In endeavouring to answer your thoughtful, well-prepared questions, they forget their shyness and even sometimes go to the other extreme and cannot stop talking, in which case, see below.

Usually, however, the interviewee's inarticulateness is more the fault of the interviewer than the interviewee. Among the mistakes the interviewer can make that may cause the interviewee to dry up are asking one closed question after another and leading the interviewee into answers the interviewer wants, for example:

'We at Bloggs & Co. like our staff to be ambitious. Are you ambitious?' Frequent leading questions will also put the interviewees under pressure, to which they may react by not answering properly or at all.

The interviewee may perceive the questions as inappropriate, irrelevant or unnecessarily intimate, and as being asked more out of curiosity than a genuine need to know, such as 'Doesn't your husband object to you going out to work with three small children to bring up?'

The interviewer's attitude or questions may bore the interviewee. A recent American study has isolated those characteristics that induce tedium in others, and they include what the psychologists call 'low affectivity', which means avoiding eye contact, keeping facial expressions to a minimum and speaking monotonously. Uninteresting questions, asked in a flat, dull voice with a glazed 'I wish this was over' expression, are bound to send the interviewee into a doze.

It is important to remember that the interviewees must feel they are getting something out of the interview over and beyond the chance of a job or the possible solution to a problem. They should feel that in meeting you and being listened to, the interview has been a rewarding experience.

We have seen already that if the interviewer seeks information that the interviewee has already supplied or goes over ground that has already been examined, the interviewee will switch off. Mature applicants are far more interested in answering questions relating to recent work experience, on which their memory is likely to be more reliable, than to questions about school or university.

The interviewee can't stop talking. Sometimes, because they are nervous, the most reluctant interviewees, once they get going, cannot stop the flow of talk. It is up to the interviewer to come to their aid, otherwise time will be wasted and the interviewer will end up with a lot of useless information.

Interviewers who are managing an interview properly will know how far to let the interviewees run on and when to rein them in. They may decide that, although the interviewees seem to be going off at a tangent, they will ultimately reveal something important, which will be worth waiting for. On the other hand, they may decide that the interviewees have said enough on that particular subject and desire to move on to the next. Politeness should not prevent you from breaking in. You have to interrupt, even if it means stopping interviewees in mid sentence, if you want to use the time available properly.

One simple way is to say, 'Yes, that's very interesting, and we may come back to it later, but now I'd like to go on to . . .' As you are suggesting that they may have a chance to continue at some later stage in the interview, the interviewees will at least be reassured that you are not dismissing what they are telling you. In the meantime, you have regained control, and the interview can continue. Whether or not you do come back to that point is up to you. As it was probably irrelevant in the first place, you may conveniently forget about it, and so will the interviewee.

If, however, the interviewees persist in chatting on, you may have to be firmer and remind them that for both of you time is precious, and you would therefore like to move on to questions you still have to ask. Remember: you are the one with the responsibility of getting the most out of the interview within the allotted time. If you take that responsibility seriously, both of you will benefit.

The interviewer does too much talking. Interviewers, do not forget, should speak no more than about fifteen per cent of the time; the rest is for the interviewees and for those important silences that can help them to formulate their responses.

The one invariable rule of interviewing is that the more talking interviewers do, the less information they obtain from the interviewee. Nervousness and lack of confidence, usually caused or exaggerated by lack of preparation, are the main reasons for this happening. Terrified of silence, the interviewer rattles on and the interviewee can hardly get a word in.

Unfortunately, interviewers do not always hear their own voices, and it is only when the interview is finished that they realize they have obtained very little useful information from the interviewee. It comes back to the need for interviewers to be able to stand outside the situation and see themselves in relationship to the interviewee. With a little practice, this skill can be perfected. If, then, you hear your own voice too much, stop, take a deep breath and let the interviewee take over the talking again, prompted, of course, by a good question from you.

The interview goes off course. This is another problem of control brought about by lack of a plan and preparation. If you go into the interview without first defining for yourself, even in the broadest terms, what you wish to get out of it and, in addition, you do not know what questions you want or need to ask, it is quite easy for the interview to deteriorate into a shambles, with neither you nor the interviewee knowing what is going on.

The simple answer is always to prepare yourself adequately, even for those interviews that you think, because you have conducted so many of them in the past, you can handle with your eyes closed. The next one may trip you up!

If, in spite of your preparation, you lose your way, you should return to the point where things started to go wrong, and no harm or loss of face will come from admitting the problem to the interviewee: 'I'm sorry, I seem to have lost my way. Now, where was I? Could we go back to . . .' In fact, the interviewee might even appreciate your admission, because it will make you appear more human and approachable.

You may not wish to go back but to move the interview on, in which case you should sum up before putting the next question. Summing up has the immediate effect of getting you back into the flow of the interview and at the same time reinforcing what the interviewee has already told you.

The interviewer allows emotions and prejudices to affect judgement. As has been remarked before, interviewers are only human; they have their likes and dislikes, their principles, their own moral standards, which may sometimes conflict with those of the interviewee. Ordinarily in an interview these should cause no trouble, but, if interviewers allow them to interfere with their objectivity, they will find it very difficult not to show by word or gesture how they feel, and that will send the interviewee diving for cover. The vital element of trust will have been lost, and to protect themselves from what they perceive as the interviewer's criticism and dis-approval, the interviewees will either give brief, inadequate answers or try very hard to win the interviewer's approval again and give only those answers they think will please.

Positive feelings about interviewees should not be hidden, because they will encourage them to be open with you; but negative feelings should. Your business is to obtain information, not to sit in judgement. You can always make your judgements and decisions after the interview is over. Until then the rule is: keep your criticisms and negative opinions to yourself.

Objectivity, confidence and maturity make the ideal inter-viewer. If you think you are lacking in one or all of these qualities, it becomes all the more important to have a plan – a general view of the issues you wish to examine in the interview. Then, if the interviewee tells you things that would otherwise shock you, for example admitting to a criminal record, you will not be led astray or distracted, because the plan is there to save you from your own embarrassment.

STAGE 5: ENDING THE INTERVIEW

ooo

How long should an interview last? Often asked, this is one of those 'piece of string' questions with no right answer, because so much depends on the type of interview. A fact-finding interview may last a few minutes, a problem-solving interview an hour or more.

A survey of employment interviews showed that the length of the interview depended on the status of the interviewees and the job they were applying for. The shortest time – about fifteen minutes – was spent interviewing unskilled workers; the longest – an hour – was with senior executives. It is arguable, however, whether fifteen minutes is long enough for any kind of employment interview, no matter who the candidate and what the job is.

Should a strict time-limit be set? Some experts argue that by doing so the interviewer will be forced to plan ahead rather than leaving anything to chance, and the interviewee will be forced to answer as fully as possible within the given time. It is thus the best way to concentrate the minds of both participants. Others argue that it creates too much stress, that it gives interviewees the impression that the interviewer has little time to spare for them and that an interview conducted under a strict time-limit produces superficial results. I suspect the truth lies somewhere between the two and is contained in the word 'flexibility'.

Assess in advance how long you expect the interview to last. A job interview, for example, may require an hour: half an hour for work history, fifteen minutes for educational qualifications, the rest for present circumstances. Inform the interviewee of the time-limit so that you both know you are working to it.

If there are matters that need to be examined in greater detail, let the interview continue until you have done so, remembering all the while to keep it moving at a brisk pace. Provided you have allowed enough time, the limit you set will create the right amount of pressure to ensure a purposeful discussion, and there should be less danger of you going off course.

No matter how much ground has to be covered, avoid driving the interviewee too fast, because you will destroy the rapport. There must be time for warming up, time for probing and time for a proper end.

When has an interview come to an end? Is it when all the necessary questions have been asked or when the allotted time has run out? What sometimes happens is that the time runs out before all the questions have been asked, because the interviewer has started off at a snail's pace and then, realizing there is a danger of over-running, makes a frantic rush to the end.

To pace the interview correctly, ensuring that it maintains a steady forward movement from start to finish:

- have a broad idea of the issues that need to be explored
- have a strategy, but be prepared to amend it where necessary
- deal with one subject before moving on to the next
- keep your interviewee interested
- keep a discreet eye on the clock, not to make the interviewees think you are anxious to see the back of them but to remind yourself that you have not unlimited time to get the information you need.

How should an interview be ended? How an interview ends is determined by the circumstances in which it was conducted and what has happened during the course of it. Depending on the type of interview, a relationship will have been established between interviewer and interviewee that may vary from remote to intense. In a problem-solving interview, for example, the interviewer may have had to probe into aspects of the interviewee's private life without, of course, becoming involved in it, and the interviewee may have had to reveal personal details that not even those closest to him or her know about. Even in a fact-finding interview, interviewer and interviewee may have become quite friendly, though it is more likely that both participants will part knowing and needing to know nothing more about each other than was covered in the interview, as when a manager interviews reps to find out what they have to sell.

Full and probing as an interview has been, it is not always possible to cover everything in one session. Job selection often takes a minimum of two interviews before the right candidate can be found. When problems have to be solved, it may take one interview to identify the problem, another to help the interviewee find a solution and a third to assess whether or not the solution has worked. Such is also the case with disciplinary interviewing. In the first interview the fault is recognized and the interviewees are given a chance to mend their ways; in the second an appraisal is made of whether or not they have done so. If they have not, a third interview for dismissal may have to follow.

When an interview is going to be followed by another, the interviewer should leave the interviewee with an idea of what happened during the interview and what is likely to happen afterwards.

For a job interview:

INTERVIEWER: As you know, this is the first interview, and, if you are short-listed, you will have to attend another interview with the director in charge of your department, who will also be testing your skills. You will be notified within the next fortnight whether or not you are on the short list, but, if you haven't heard from us by then, you must assume, I'm afraid, that you're not.

The discipline or problem-solving interview:

INTERVIEWER: I don't think we can take it further than that for the moment. We've agreed that you'll try to change your attitude and put more into your work for the next two months, and we will review the situation after that.

Whatever the interview, there are some general rules about ending it. Firstly, be courteous and friendly. There really should be no need to mention this, but sometimes, in the rush to end the interview, it is only too easy to dismiss interviewees in a way that they may interpret as off-hand and discourteous. After all, it costs nothing to be nice. A simple 'Thank you for coming along, I enjoyed meeting you' is much to be preferred to the 'Don't call us, we'll call you' routine.

For the disappointed job applicants, who are probably feeling anxious enough as it is, ending on a positive note and with a gentle let-down will preserve their self-esteem and reflect well not only on you but on the organization you represent. And, who knows, you may still want them at a later stage, either for the job they applied for or another one.

INTERVIEWER: I've been impressed by your qualifications and what you've told me about yourself, but, as you probably know, we've had many applicants for this post, so I don't want to raise your hopes . . .

Secondly, be businesslike. You can be polite and businesslike at the same time; the one does not exclude the other. Neither you nor the interviewee wants to prolong the interview beyond its span, so bring it to an end when you think it is appropriate to do so, even if you still have time left over. Give the interviewees the opportunity to ask questions or make comments on anything that has been dealt with or on matters that may still bother them. Don't assume they will do so uninvited; you have to issue the invitation.

INTERVIEWER: Is there anything more you'd like to add to what we covered? Would you like to ask me any questions about the job or the company?

Interviewees who have come to you with a problem or for a disciplinary matter ought to be left knowing that your interest is a continuing one that does not stop the moment they leave your office. A businesslike way of ending such interviews is to agree on some future action and, if possible, arrange a follow-up meeting.

You must not leave them with the idea that you will take the problem over and solve it or that in a disciplinary interview talk takes the place of action and that they have nothing more to do. On the contrary, if the interview has been successful, they ought to be in a far better position to understand their difficulties and to know how to deal with them.

INTERVIEWER: Well, I'm glad we've had this talk and that you now know what to do. Please let me know how things turn out.

Whatever technique you employ to end the interview:
- never take upon yourself the interviewees' problems by saying, 'Leave it to me. I'll handle it'
- never pretend to be in a position to make decisions that affect their future if you are not. If your assessment of the candidates has to go to a higher authority, don't let them think you can decide whether they have got the job or not
- never give interviewees false hopes.

Athletes know that good exercise depends on proper warming up and proper winding down. It's the same with the interview. Put your interviewees in the right frame of mind at the start by a positive, friendly approach. Show that you are glad to see them and that you want to get the most out of the interview for both their sake and yours. At the end of the interview thank them for giving up their time (even if it is essentially *your* time and for *their* benefit), express your interest in what has been said and let them feel that it has been worthwhile, whatever the results.

Part 3: Summing Up

TWENTY WAYS TO SUCCESSFUL INTERVIEWING

ooo

Interviewing is not easy, and for most of us it does not come naturally. A little guidance, I believe, can go a long way to overcome some of the most obvious errors that interviewers make, errors that can adversely affect the lives and careers of both interviewers and interviewees.

Whatever their nature or subject-matter, most interviews follow a similar plan. What I have set out to do in this short book is to analyse that plan, highlighting its most important elements, so that interviewers, experienced and inexperienced, may gain some useful insights on how to proceed with greater confidence, thereby reducing the chances of making unnecessary mistakes. For more experienced interviewers there may be satisfaction in confirming that what they have been doing instinctively all along is probably correct.

To sum up, here are twenty suggestions on how to improve your interviewing skills.

1. Every interview has a purpose. Make sure you know what you want from your interview and frame your questions accordingly.

2. Scout motto: be prepared. Muddling through is inefficient and time-wasting. Find out what you can about the interviewee (from the application form, for example), so that questions can be directed to new areas of interest.

3. Jot down your main questions beforehand and have them near you in the interview. It acts as a script to guide you, but

you do not have to stick strictly to it. So long as you stay within the agreed limits of discussion and maintain a logical shape to the interview, go where the answers lead.

4. Ensure that you are not likely to be interrupted and that the interview room is free from distractions, like noise and bright lights. Chairs should be arranged so that you can see and hear each other without strain. Sitting with a small table between you, rather than a large desk separating you, is congenial without being too intimate.

5. Greet the interviewees in a friendly, polite, open manner, if possible going out of your office to meet them, and cultivate a line in non-threatening, casual chat to put them at ease.

6. Take control from the start and maintain it throughout. This does not mean bullying, nor does it mean arguing or debating with the interviewees. Your opinions are irrelevant. You want to know what they think and feel.

7. Guide the interviewees by giving them an overall idea of what subjects are going to be covered and ask questions that encourage them to talk freely. Except for factual information, avoid questions that require only a one-word reply.

8. Remember: it is an interview not an interrogation, so avoid multiple questions, trick questions and leading questions that force interviewees to answer in the way you want rather than the way they want.

9. Speak clearly, using a friendly, reassuring tone, and at a volume the interviewees can hear without straining or becoming deafened.

10. Aim to achieve a good rapport with the interviewees. Let them do most of the talking and show by voice, facial expression and gesture that you are interested in what they are telling you. Keep your own feelings of likes or dislikes and approval or disapproval to yourself.

11. Develop the art of good listening. This means concentrating on what the interviewees are telling you, showing them that

you are doing so and also 'hearing' what the interviewees convey by gestures and expression.

12. Keep eye contact, but do not stare in a threatening or intimate manner.

13. Do not be frightened of silences. Pauses between questions indicate that interviewees have more to say. Do not rush them and give them the chance to answer you in full.

14. Maintain a steady, unhurried pace and be systematic in completing each section of the interview before moving on to the next.

15. Do not be scared to ask difficult, searching questions. If the interviewees become hostile or emotional, do not lose your temper but maintain a calm detachment and try to distract them by concentrating on the facts rather than the feelings.

16. If the interviewees become upset, do not be tempted to act the psychiatrist. Your role is to ask questions and, by listening to what they tell you, to help them to articulate their problems and find their own solutions.

17. Avoid all unnecessary and irrelevant references to the interviewee's appearance, sex, age, religion or race.

18. Short-term memory is unreliable, so take notes. Keep them brief and try not to lose eye contact for too long while you are doing so.

19. Interviews should not be open-ended. Work to a time-limit, as it helps concentrate the mind. If you are conducting a number of interviews on one day and are running late, do not forget to apologize personally to those who are waiting. Better still, offer them a cup of coffee.

20. End the interview in the same friendly manner in which it began and, no matter what the nature of the interview, always try to leave your interviewees with their dignity and self-esteem intact.

A CHOICE OF PENGUINS AND PELICANS

Lateral Thinking for Management Edward de Bono

Creativity and lateral thinking can work together for managers in developing new products or ideas; Edward de Bono shows how.

Understanding Organizations Charles B. Handy

Of practical as well as theoretical interest, this book shows how general concepts can help solve specific organizational problems.

The Art of Japanese Management Richard Tanner Pascale and Anthony G. Athos With an Introduction by Sir Peter Parker

Japanese industrial success owes much to Japanese management techniques, which we in the West neglect at our peril. The lessons are set out in this important book.

My Years with General Motors Alfred P. Sloan With an Introduction by John Egan

A business classic by the man who took General Motors to the top – and kept them there for decades.

Introducing Management Ken Elliott and Peter Lawrence (eds.)

An important and comprehensive collection of texts on modern management which draw some provocative conclusions.

English Culture and the Decline of the Industrial Spirit Martin J. Wiener

A major analysis of why the 'world's first industrial nation has never been comfortable with industrialism'. 'Very persuasive' – Anthony Sampson in the *Observer*

Dinosaur and Co   Tom Lloyd

A lively and optimistic survey of a new breed of businessmen who are breaking away from huge companies to form dynamic enterprises in microelectronics, biotechnology and other developing areas.

The Money Machine: How the City Works   Philip Coggan

How are the big deals made? Which are the institutions that *really* matter? What causes the pound to rise or interest rates to fall? This book provides clear and concise answers to these and many other money-related questions.

Parkinson's Law   C. Northcote Parkinson

'Work expands so as to fill the time available for its completion': that law underlies this 'extraordinarily funny and witty book' (Stephen Potter in the *Sunday Times*) which also makes some painfully serious points for those in business or the Civil Service.

Debt and Danger   Harold Lever and Christopher Huhne

The international debt crisis was brought about by Western bankers in search of quick profit and is now one of our most pressing problems. This book looks at the background and shows what we must do to avoid disaster.

Lloyd's Bank Tax Guide 1987/8

Cut through the complexities! Work the system in *your* favour! Don't pay a penny more than you have to! Written for anyone who has to deal with personal tax, this up-to-date and concise new handbook includes all the important changes in this year's budget.

The Spirit of Enterprise   George Gilder

A lucidly written and excitingly argued defence of capitalism and the role of the entrepreneur within it.

PENGUIN BUSINESS AND ECONOMICS

Almost Everyone's Guide to Economics
J. K. Galbraith and Nicole Salinger

This instructive and entertaining dialogue provides a step-by-step explanation of 'the state of economics in general and the reasons for its present failure in particular in simple, accurate language that everyone could understand and that a perverse few might conceivably enjoy'.

The Rise and Fall of Monetarism   David Smith

Now that even Conservatives have consigned monetarism to the scrapheap of history, David Smith draws out the unhappy lessons of a fundamentally flawed economic experiment, driven by a doctrine that for years had been regarded as outmoded and irrelevant.

Atlas of Management Thinking   Edward de Bono

This fascinating book provides a vital repertoire of non-verbal images that will help activate the right side of any manager's brain.

The Economist Economics   Rupert Pennant-Rea and Clive Crook

Based on a series of 'briefs' published in *The Economist*, this is a clear and accessible guide to the key issues of today's economics for the general reader.

Understanding Organizations   Charles B. Handy

Of practical as well as theoretical interest, this book shows how general concepts can help solve specific organizational problems.

The Winning Streak   Walter Goldsmith and David Clutterbuck

A brilliant analysis of what Britain's best-run and most successful companies have in common – a must for all managers.

A CHOICE OF PENGUINS

The Secret Lives of Trebitsch Lincoln   Bernard Wasserstein

Trebitsch Lincoln was Member of Parliament, international spy, right-wing revolutionary, Buddhist monk – and this century's most extraordinary conman. 'Surely the final work on a truly extraordinary career' – Hugh Trevor-Roper. 'An utterly improbable story ... a biographical coup' – *Guardian*

Out of Africa   Karen Blixen (Isak Dinesen)

After the failure of her coffee-farm in Kenya, where she lived from 1913 to 1931, Karen Blixen went home to Denmark and wrote this unforgettable account of her experiences. 'No reader can put the book down without some share in the author's poignant farewell to her farm' – *Observer*

In My Wildest Dreams   Leslie Thomas

The autobiography of Leslie Thomas, author of *The Magic Army* and *The Dearest and the Best*. From Barnardo boy to original virgin soldier, from apprentice journalist to famous novelist, it is an amazing story. 'Hugely enjoyable' – *Daily Express*

The Winning Streak   Walter Goldsmith and David Clutterbuck

Marks and Spencer, Saatchi and Saatchi, United Biscuits, GEC ... The UK's top companies reveal their formulas for success, in an important and stimulating book that no British manager can afford to ignore.

Bird of Life, Bird of Death   Jonathan Evan Maslow

In the summer of 1983 Jonathan Maslow set out to find the quetzal. In doing so, he placed himself between the natural and unnatural histories of Central America, between the vulnerable magnificence of nature and the terrible destructiveness of man. 'A wonderful book' – *The New York Times Book Review*

Mob Star   Gene Mustain and Jerry Capeci

Handsome, charming, deadly, John Gotti is the real-life Mafia boss at the head of New York's most feared criminal family. *Mob Star* tells the chilling and compelling story of the rise to power of the most powerful criminal in America.

FOR THE BEST IN PAPERBACKS, LOOK FOR THE 🐧

A CHOICE OF PENGUINS

The Assassination of Federico García Lorca   Ian Gibson

Lorca's 'crime' was his antipathy to pomposity, conformity and intolerance. His punishment was murder. Ian Gibson – author of the acclaimed new biography of Lorca – reveals the truth about his death and the atmosphere in Spain that allowed it to happen.

Between the Woods and the Water   Patrick Leigh Fermor

Patrick Leigh Fermor continues his celebrated account – begun in *A Time of Gifts* – of his journey on foot from the Hook of Holland to Constantinople. 'Even better than everyone says it is' – Peter Levi. 'Indescribably rich and beautiful' – *Guardian*

The Hunting of the Whale   Jeremy Cherfas

'*The Hunting of the Whale* is a story of declining profits and mounting pigheadedness ... it involves a catalogue of crass carelessness ... Jeremy Cherfas brings a fresh eye to [his] material ... for anyone wanting a whale in a nutshell this must be the book to choose' – *The Times Literary Supplement*

Metamagical Themas   Douglas R. Hofstadter

This astonishing sequel to the bestselling, Pulitzer Prize-winning *Gödel, Escher, Bach* swarms with 'extraordinary ideas, brilliant fables, deep philosophical questions and Carrollian word play' – Martin Gardner

Into the Heart of Borneo   Redmond O'Hanlon

'Perceptive, hilarious and at the same time a serious natural-history journey into one of the last remaining unspoilt paradises' – *New Statesman*. 'Consistently exciting, often funny and erudite without ever being overwhelming' – *Punch*

When the Wind Blows   Raymond Briggs

'A visual parable against nuclear war: all the more chilling for being in the form of a strip cartoon' – *Sunday Times*. 'The most eloquent anti-Bomb statement you are likely to read' – *Daily Mail*

A CHOICE OF PENGUINS

Better Together   Christian Partnership in a Hurt City
David Sheppard and Derek Warlock

The Anglican and Roman Catholic Bishops of Liverpool tell the uplifting and heartening story of their alliance in the fight for their city – an alliance that has again and again reached out to heal a community torn by sectarian loyalties and bitter deprivation.

Fantastic Invasion   Patrick Marnham

Explored and exploited, Africa has carried a different meaning for each wave of foreign invaders – from ivory traders to aid workers. Now, in the crisis that has followed Independence, which way should Africa turn? 'A courageous and brilliant effort' – Paul Theroux

Jean Rhys: Letters 1931–66
Edited by Francis Wyndham and Diana Melly

'Eloquent and invaluable … her life emerges, and with it a portrait of an unexpectedly indomitable figure' – Marina Warner in the *Sunday Times*

Among the Russians   Colin Thubron

One man's solitary journey by car across Russia provides an enthralling and revealing account of the habits and idiosyncrasies of a fascinating people. 'He sees things with the freshness of an innocent and the erudition of a scholar' – *Daily Telegraph*

They Went to Portugal   Rose Macaulay

An exotic and entertaining account of travellers to Portugal from the pirate-crusaders, through poets, aesthetes and ambassadors, to the new wave of romantic travellers. A wonderful mixture of literature, history and adventure, by one of our most stylish and seductive writers.

The Separation Survival Handbook   Helen Garlick

Separation and divorce almost inevitably entail a long journey through a morass of legal, financial, custodial and emotional problems. Stripping the experience of both jargon and guilt, marital lawyer Helen Garlick maps clearly the various routes that can be taken.

A CHOICE OF PENGUINS

The Russian Album   Michael Ignatieff

Michael Ignatieff movingly comes to terms with the meaning of his own family's memories and histories, in a book that is both an extraordinary account of the search for roots and a dramatic and poignant chronicle of four generations of a Russian family.

Beyond the Blue Horizon   Alexander Frater

The romance and excitement of the legendary Imperial Airways East-bound Empire service – the world's longest and most adventurous scheduled air route – relived fifty years later in one of the most original travel books of the decade. 'The find of the year' – *Today*

Getting to Know the General   Graham Greene

'In August 1981 my bag was packed for my fifth visit to Panama when the news came to me over the telephone of the death of General Omar Torrijos Herrera, my friend and host...' 'Vigorous, deeply felt, at times funny, and for Greene surprisingly frank' – *Sunday Times*

The Search for the Virus   Steve Connor and Sharon Kingman

In this gripping book, two leading *New Scientist* journalists tell the remarkable story of how researchers discovered the AIDS virus and examine the links between AIDS and lifestyles. They also look at the progress being made in isolating the virus and finding a cure.

Arabian Sands   Wilfred Thesiger

'In the tradition of Burton, Doughty, Lawrence, Philby and Thomas, it is, very likely, the book about Arabia to end all books about Arabia' – *Daily Telegraph*

Adieux: A Farewell to Sartre   Simone de Beauvoir

A devastatingly frank account of the last years of Sartre's life, and his death, by the woman who for more than half a century shared that life. 'A true labour of love, there is about it a touching sadness, a mingling of the personal with the impersonal and timeless which Sartre himself would surely have liked and understood' – *Listener*

FOR THE BEST IN PAPERBACKS, LOOK FOR THE

PENGUIN REFERENCE BOOKS

The Penguin Guide to the Law

This acclaimed reference book is designed for everyday use and forms the most comprehensive handbook ever published on the law as it affects the individual.

The Penguin Medical Encyclopedia

Covers the body and mind in sickness and in health, including drugs, surgery, medical history, medical vocabulary and many other aspects. 'Highly commendable' – *Journal of the Institute of Health Education*

The Slang Thesaurus

Do you make the public bar sound like a gentleman's club? Do you need help in understanding *Minder*? The miraculous *Slang Thesaurus* will liven up your language in no time. You won't Adam and Eve it! A mine of funny, witty, acid and vulgar synonyms for the words you use every day.

The Penguin Dictionary of Troublesome Words   Bill Bryson

Why should you avoid discussing the *weather conditions*? Can a married woman be *celibate*? Why is it eccentric to talk about the *aroma* of a cowshed? A straightforward guide to the pitfalls and hotly disputed issues in standard written English.

A Dictionary of Literary Terms

Defines over 2,000 literary terms (including lesser known, foreign language and technical terms), explained with illustrations from literature past and present.

The Concise Cambridge Italian Dictionary

Compiled by Barbara Reynolds, this work is notable for the range of examples provided to illustrate the exact meaning of Italian words and phrases. It also contains a pronunciation guide and a reference grammar.